THE RIVER NIGER

The River Niger

A PLAY BY
Joseph A. Walker

A MERMAID DRAMABOOK

Hill and Wang   New York

A DIVISION OF FARRAR, STRAUS AND GIROUX

This play is dedicated to my mother and father and to highly underrated black daddies everywhere.

Joe Walker's Autobiography

Born 6:44 p.m. on February 24, 1935, under the sun sign of Pisces, moon in Scorpio, rising—Leo—Virgo via a Cancer mother and an I-don't-remember-what-sign daddy, who was a bad-loud-talking dude of five feet eight inches tall, whom I once saw beat up a man six foot five because he insulted my seven-year-old dignity by beating the daylights out of me on account of I and my buddies were on a hate-little-girls campaign, throwing bottle tops at the cutest little brown-oak girl with skinny legs and a yellow ribbon on her greased ponytail, whom I don't think I really hated in retrospect because of her almond-shaped eyes—anyway, my pop was some dude—used to sleep out on the back porch in the dead of winter because he didn't want Ma to know he was drunk, because my ma, man, was a scornful bitter-sweet lovable crazy lady who was not quite as sweet as Mattie in *The River Niger* but who was pretty goddamn sweet and *giving* anyway, who once hit me over my head with the heel of her shoe, chasing me all the way from the dining room to my bedroom on account of I said Grandma was not the nicest person in the world—Ma didn't allow nobody to talk about her mama; no, man, and I can dig it. I started to become a professional philosopher, whatever that means, changed my mind on account of I got what you may stuffily call an artistic temperament and I like to do my thinking through plays and things—who am I, who am I, why, I'm Joe Walker—here today, gone tomorrow, yet somehow eternal— If you can see your way clear to call yourself God, I will allow you to call me the same—otherwise, the universe is doing its thing—leave the mother alone. I love lions 'cause they is so, so motherf—so mother-fu—so goddamn motherfucking sweet!

The River Niger was first performed by the Negro Ensemble Company, Inc., New York City, December 5, 1972. On March 27, 1973, it opened at the Brooks Atkinson Theatre, New York City. The cast for both presentations was as follows:

JOHN WILLIAMS	*Douglas Turner Ward*
MATTIE WILLIAMS	*Roxie Roker*
GRANDMA WILHEMINA BROWN	*Frances Foster*
DR. DUDLEY STANTON	*Graham Brown*
JEFF WILLIAMS	*Les Roberts*
ANN VANDERGUILD	*Grenna Whitaker*
MO	*Neville Richen*
GAIL	*Saundra McClain*
CHIPS	*Lennal Wainwright*
AL	*Dean Irby*
SKEETER	*Charles Weldon*

THE RIVER NIGER

Characters

JOHN WILLIAMS *in his fifties, an alive poet*

MATTIE WILLIAMS *in her fifties, an embittered but happy woman*

GRANDMA WILHEMINA BROWN *eighty-two, very alive, Mattie's mother*

DR. DUDLEY STANTON *in his fifties, cynical, classic Jamaican, lover of poetry*

JEFF WILLIAMS *twenty-five, John's son, thoughtful, wild, a credit to his father*

ANN VANDERGUILD *twenty-two, strong black South African girl, lover of quality*

MO *twenty-four, young black leader of underlying beauty and integrity*

GAIL *twenty-one, very much in love with Mo*

MO'S MEN:

CHIPS *sexually perverted, a young fool*

AL *the closet homosexual, capable, determined, very young*

SKEETER *basically good, but hung on dope*

LIEUTENANT STAPLES *police officer (voice only)*

BASS PLAYER *highly skillful at creating a mood (not seen), provides musical poetry for the play*

Act One

TIME: February 1, the Present: 4:30 p.m.

PLACE: New York City—Harlem.

SETTING: *Brownstone on 133rd between Lenox and Seventh. Living room and kitchen cross section. Living room a subdued green. Modest living-room suite consisting of coffee table, two easy chairs, and a sofa. The chairs and sofa are covered with transparent plastic slipcovers. There is a television set with its back to the audience.*

The kitchen is almost as large as the living room. There are a large kitchen table and four chairs. Stage right is an entrance from the back porch to the kitchen. Stage left is an entrance that leads from a small vestibule to a hallway —to the living room. In the hallway is a stairway that leads upstairs.

The house is not luxuriously decorated, of course, but it is not garish either. The "attempt" is to be cozy. Even

*though the place is very clean, there are many magazines
and old newspapers around—giving the general appear-
ance of casual "clutter."*

(*At rise, a bass counterpoint creeps in, and* GRANDMA WIL-
HEMINA BROWN, *a stately, fair-skinned black woman in her
middle eighties is in the kitchen. She is humming "Rock
of Ages" and pouring herself an oversized cup of coffee.
She drops in two teaspoons of sugar and a fraction of cream,
which she returns to the refrigerator. For a moment she
stops humming and looks around stealthily. She goes to the
kitchen window and peeps out into the backyard. Satisfied
that she is alone, she opens the cabinet under the sink.
With one final furtive glance around, she reaches under
the cabinet and feels about till she finds what she's been
looking for—a bottle of Old Grand-dad. Apparently, she
unhooks it from under the top of the cabinet, glances
around once more, then pours an extremely generous por-
tion into her coffee. There is a sound from the back yard—
as if someone or something has brushed by a trash can. She
freezes for a second. With unbelievable speed she "hooks"
the bottle back into her secret hiding place, snatches her
coffee, and hurries out of the kitchen.* GRANDMA *pauses on
the stairs. In the next moment we hear a key in the back
door.* GRANDMA *hurries out of view. The back door opens
cautiously. It is* JOHN WILLIAMS, *a thin, medium-sized
brown man in his middle fifties. His hair is gray at the
temples and slicked down. He has a salt-and-pepper mus-
tache. He wears a brown topcoat, combat boots, corduroy
pants—on his head a heavily crusted painter's cap. He is
obviously intoxicated but very much in control. From his
topcoat pocket he removes a bottle of Johnnie Walker Red*

Label, which he opens, and takes a long swallow, grimacing as he does so. He then stuffs the bottle into his "hiding place," behind the refrigerator. He pushes the refrigerator back in place and removes his topcoat. Pulling out his wallet, he begins counting its contents. Extremely dissatisfied with the count, he sits heavily and ponders his plight. A second later he takes out a piece of paper.)

JOHN

(Reading aloud to himself as bass line comes back in.)
I am the River Niger—hear my waters.
I wriggle and stream and run.
I am totally flexible—
Damn!
(He crumples the paper and stuffs it into his pants pocket. In the very next instant, he remembers something—goes out the back door and returns with a small cedar jewelry box which he places on the table with great pride. There is a rapping at the back door. Bass fades out. JOHN *is startled. He begins sneaking out of the room when he hears . . .)*

VOICE

(Softly but intensely)
Johnny Williams! Open the damn door.
(Raps again.)
It's me, Dudley. Open up!
*(*JOHN *goes to the door.)*
It's Dudley Stanton, fool.
*(*JOHN *opens the door.* DUDLEY STANTON, *a thin, wiry, very dark black man—in his late fifties—graying. He is impeccably but conservatively dressed. The two men stare at each other. Much love flows between them.)*

JOHN
Well, I'll be a son-of-a-bitch.

DUDLEY
(*In a thick and beautiful Jamaican accent*)
Yeah, man, that's what you are, a son-of-a-bitch. Now, will
a son-of-a-bitch let a son-of-a-whore in? It's very cold out
here, man! Did I ever tell you my ma was a whore?

JOHN
Only a thousand times. Come on in, ya monkey chaser.

DUDLEY
(*Coming in.*)
Now, you know I can't stand that expression. Why do you
want to burden our friendship with that expression?

JOHN
Where in the hell you been?

DUDLEY
Can I take off my coat first?

JOHN
Take off your jockstrap for all I care. Where in the hell
you been?

DUDLEY
To Mexico on vacation—fishing, man. And oh, what fish-
ing. Man, I tell you.

JOHN
Did it ever occur to you that your old buddy might like to
go fishing too? Did that ever cross your mind?

DUDLEY
You ain't never got no vacation time coming. You use it up faster than you earn it.

JOHN
Well, at least you could have let a buddy know you were going.
(*Sees the bottle under* DUDLEY's *arm.*)
Give me a drink?

DUDLEY
Sure thing.
(*Hands* JOHN *the bottle.*)

JOHN
Vodka! I be damned! You know I can't stand vodka.

DUDLEY
You don't want my vodka, go on behind the refrig and get your Scotch. I saw you hide it there.

JOHN
You been spying on me with that damn telescope again.

DUDLEY
Yeah. I saw you coming in. Closed my office.

JOHN
You old monkey chaser.

DUDLEY
One day, I'm going to brain you for that expression.

JOHN
Goddamn black Jew doctor. You make all the money in the world and you can't even buy your poor buddy a bottle of Scotch.

DUDLEY
Hell, I shouldn't even drink with you.
(*Pause.*)
If you don't stop boozing the way you do, you'll be dead
in five years. You're killing yourself bit by bit, Johnny.

JOHN
Well, that's a helluva sight better than doing it all at once.
Besides, I can stop any time I want to.

DUDLEY
Then why don't you?

JOHN
I don't want to.
(*Changing the subject purposely.*)
Dudley, my son's due home tomorrow.

DUDLEY
Jeff coming home? No lie! That's wonderful! Old Jeff.
Let's take a run up to the Big Apple and celebrate!

JOHN
That's where I'm coming from. I left work early today—I
got so damned worked up, you know. I mean, all I could
see was my boy—big-time first lieutenant in the United
States of America Air Force—Strategic Air Command—
navigator—walking through the front door with them bars
—them shining silver bars on his goddamn shoulders.
(*He begins saluting an imaginary Jeff.*)
Yes, sir. Whatever you say, sir. Right away, Lieutenant
Williams. Lieutenant Jeff Williams.

DUDLEY
Johnny Williams, you are the biggest fool in God's crea-

tion. How in the name of your grandma's twat could you get so worked up over the white man's air force? I've always said, "That's what's wrong with these American niggers. They believe anything that has a little tinsel sprinkled on it." "Shining silver bars." Fantasy, man!

JOHN
He's my son, Dudley, and I'm proud of him.

DUDLEY
You're supposed to be, but because he managed to survive this syphilitic asshole called Harlem, not because he's a powerless nub in a silly military grist mill. What you use for brains, man?

JOHN
I'm a fighter, Dudley. I don't like white folks either, but I sure do love their war machines. I'm a fighter who ain't got no battlefield. I woke up one day, looked around, and said to myself, "There's a war going on, but where's the battlefield?" I'm gonna find it one day—you watch.

DUDLEY
In other words, you'd gladly give your life for your poor downtrodden black brothers and sisters if you only knew where to give it?

JOHN
Right! For my people!

DUDLEY
I wonder how many niggers have said those words: "For my people!"

JOHN
Give me the right time and I'd throw this rubbish on the
rubbish heap in a minute.

DUDLEY
Cop-out! That's all that is!

JOHN
Ya goddamn monkey chaser—you're the cop-out!

DUDLEY
Cop-out! The battlefield's everywhere. That's what's
wrong with niggers in America—everybody's waiting for
the time. I don't delude myself, nigger. I know that there's
no heroism in death—just death, dirty nasty death.
(*Pours another drink.*)
The rest is jive, man! Black people are jive. The most un-
realistic, unphilosophical people in the world.

JOHN
Philosophy be damned. Give me a program—a program!

DUDLEY
A program!?! We're just fools, Johnny, white and black
retarded children, playing with matches. We don't have
the slightest idea what we're doing. Do you know, I no
longer believe in medicine. Of all man's presumptions
medicine is the most arrogantly presumptuous. People are
supposed to die! It's natural to die. If I find that a patient
has a serious disease, I send him to one of my idealistic
colleagues. I ain't saving no lives, man. I treat the hypo-
chondriacs. I treat colds, hemorrhoids, sore throats. I dis-
tribute sugar pills and run my fingers up the itching va-

ginas of sex-starved old bitches.\Women who're all dried
up, past menopause—but groping for life. They pretend
to be unmoved, but I feel their wrigglings on my fingers.
I see 'em swoon with ecstasy the deeper I probe. Liars—
every one of them who would never admit their lives are
up—what they really want is a good dose of M and M.

JOHN
M and M?

DUDLEY
Male meat! Old biddies clinging to life like tenants in
condemned houses, and medicine keeps on finding cures.
Ridiculous! Nature has a course. Let her take it!

JOHN
But what I do is part of nature's course, ya idiot!

DUDLEY
Go on, Johnny, be a hero and a black leader, and die with
a Molotov cocktail in your hand, screaming, "Power to the
People." The only value your death will have is to dent
the population explosion. You can't change your shitting
habits, let alone the world.

JOHN
You know what your trouble is, Dudley? You're just float-
ing, man, floating downwind like a silly daisy.

DUDLEY
Come on! What the hell are you rooted to?

JOHN
To the battlefield. To my people, man!

DUDLEY
You ain't got no people, nigger. Just a bunch of black crabs
in a barrel, lying to each other, always lying and pulling
each other back down.

JOHN
Who do you suppose made us that way?

DUDLEY
You want me to say *whitey,* don't you?

JOHN
Who else?

DUDLEY
You goddamn idealists kill me. You really do, you know.
No matter what the *cause* is, the fact remains that we *are*
crabs in a barrel. Now deal with that, nigger!

JOHN
Aw, go screw yourself.

DUDLEY
There you go. Hate the truth, don't you? The truth is,
you're a dying wino nigger who's trying to find some reason
for living. And now you're going to put that burden on
your son. Poor Jeff! Doesn't know what he's in for.

JOHN
(*Pause.*)
The fact remains, monkey-chasing son-of-a-bitch, the fact
remains that I got a son coming home from the air force
tomorrow and you ain't got nobody—
(*A loving afterthought.*)
but me—

DUDLEY
You are a big fool! Jessie wanted children. Every time she missed her period, I'd give her something to start it over again. Poor lovable bitch, till the day she died she never knew. But I knew—I knew it was a heinous crime to bring any more children into this pile of horse shit.

JOHN
You're sick, you know that, monkey chaser—sick. To satisfy your own perverted outlook, you'd destroy your wife's right to motherhood. Sick!

DUDLEY
. . . The day Jessie died she made me promise I'd marry again and have children, and I lied to her—told her I would— Didn't make her dying any easier, though. She still died twitching and convulsing, saliva running from the corners of her mouth—death phlegm rattling in her throat. She still died gruesomely. That's the way it is. That's life! I'm the last of my line—thank God. No more suffering for the Stantons. Thank God—that cruel son-of-a-bitch.

JOHN
You depress the shit out of me, you know that, monkey chaser—but you can still be my friend, even if you're just a chickenhearted rabbit, afraid to make a motion.

DUDLEY
(Genuinely angry.)
Look, nigger—any motion you make is on a treadmill.

JOHN
Aw, drink ya drink. What's the matter with you? It don't

take no genius to figure out that none of this shit's gonna
matter a hundred years from now—that the whole thing's
a game of musical chairs—so what? What's your favorite
word—presumptuous? Well, man, it is presumptuous as
hell of you to even think you can figure this shit out.

DUDLEY
Ain't that what we're here for, stupid? What we've got
brains for? To figure it out?

JOHN
Hell no! To play a better game, fool. Just play the mother-
fucker, that's all. And right now the game is Free My Peo-
ple. Ya get that! And if you don't play it, nigger, you know
what you're gonna become—what you *are*—you know
what you are, Dr. Dudley Stanton? You're a goddamn
spiritual vegetable. Thinking's for idiots—wise men act;
thinking is all dribble anyhow, and idiots can do a helluva
damn better job at it than you can. My advice to you, Mr.
Monkey Chaser, is fart, piss, screw, eat, fight, run, beat
your meat, sympathize, and criticize, but for God's sake,
stop thinking. It's the white folks' sickness.

DUDLEY
I'm talking to a bloody amoeba.

JOHN
Amoebas are the foundation, man, and they ain't got no
blood. Now loan me one hundred and ninety dollars.

DUDLEY
What?

JOHN
A hundred and ninety dollars—shit. Don't I speak clearly?
I had two years of college, you know.

DUDLEY
You drank all your money away?

JOHN
Hell yes.

DUDLEY
At the Apple?

JOHN
Right!

DUDLEY
Setting up everybody and his ma?

JOHN
Uh huh!

DUDLEY
Bragging like a nigger about how your first lieutenant, Air
Force, Strategic Air Command son is due home tomorrow?

JOHN
Right!

DUDLEY
And they all smiled, patted you on your back, and ordered
two more rounds of three-for-one bar slop?

JOHN
Right, nigger. Now, do I get the bread or not— Shit, I
ain't required to give you my life story for a measly hand-
out—

DUDLEY
Of a hundred and ninety dollars—

JOHN
Shit! Right!

DUDLEY
You already owe me three hundred and forty.

JOHN
That much?

DUDLEY
(*Takes out a small notebook.*)
See for yourself—

JOHN
Well, a hundred and ninety more won't break you. Do I
get it or not?
(*There is a knock on the front door.*)
Come on, man, that's Mattie.

DUDLEY
Well, well, well, look at the great warrior now—about to
get his ass kicked!

JOHN
Come on! Yes or no?

DUDLEY
But here's your battlefield, man. Start fighting! I tell you
one thing though, I'm putting my money on Mattie, man.
(*Again there is a knock on the front door.*)

JOHN
See ya later.
(*Starts for the back door.*)

DUDLEY
Wait a minute! If it were Mattie, she'd use her key, right?

JOHN
(*Comes back.*)
Hey, yeah, that's right. Didn't think of that!

DUDLEY
You don't believe in thinking.
(JOHN *goes to door and sneaks a look through the pane.*)

JOHN
(*Comes back.*)
Hey, it's a young chick. Good legs—like she might have a halfway decent turd cutter on her.

DUDLEY
Let her in, man, let her in!

JOHN
Look—am I going to get the money?

DUDLEY
(*Interrupting him.*)
We'll talk about it. I ain't saying yes and I ain't saying no.

JOHN
Sadistic bastard!
(*A more insistent knock.*)

DUDLEY
Open the goddamn door, nigger!
(JOHN *opens the door.* ANN VANDERGUILD—*a very attractive black woman in her early twenties—enters. She sparkles on top of a deep brooding inner core. A bass line of beautiful melancholy comes in.*)

JOHN
Yes, ma'am.

ANN
I'm Ann—

JOHN
Uh huh.

ANN
I'm a friend of Jeff Williams's. This, uh, is his, where he lives, isn't it?

JOHN
When he's home, yes. He won't be here until noon to-morrow.

ANN
Yes, I know—may I come in?

JOHN
Oh, I'm sorry. Come in.

ANN
Would you help me with my suitcases? They're in the cab.

JOHN
Suitcases!

ANN
Yes, I'd like to spend the night—if I may.

JOHN
Spend the night—

DUDLEY
(*Coming in from the kitchen.*)
Go get the young lady's suitcases, man. And close the damn
door. It's colder than a virgin's—
(*Catches himself.*)

JOHN
Suitcases!
(JOHN *exits.* DUDLEY *and* ANN *size each other up.*)

DUDLEY
Come on in. Let me have your coat.

ANN
Thank you.

DUDLEY
So you're Jeff's intended?

ANN
Well, not exactly, sir. We're very good friends, though.

DUDLEY
But you intend to make yourself Jeff's intended. Am I
right?
(ANN *smiles.*)
What a nice smile! Then I am right. Have a seat—
(JOHN *staggers into the room with an armful of suitcases,
plops them down, stares at* ANN *for a second. Bass fades.*)

JOHN
There's more.
(*Exits.*)

DUDLEY
Planning a long stay?

ANN
I'll go to a hotel tomorrow.

DUDLEY
I wasn't saying that for that. I'm merely intrigued with
your determination. Young women—strong-willed young
women—always fascinate me.
(JOHN enters with a small trunk on his back which he un-
loads heavily.)

JOHN
That'll be three dollars and fifty cents, young lady.

DUDLEY
I've got it, Miss— What's your last name?

ANN
Vanderguild.

DUDLEY
Miss Vanderguild.

ANN
I wouldn't think of it.

DUDLEY
(Hurriedly pays JOHN, who is somewhat bewildered.)
I told you about my weakness for strong women. My
mother was strong. Lord, how strong. Could work all day
and half the night.

JOHN
Flat on her back! Anybody can do that.

DUDLEY
Only a strong woman, man. Besides, who says she was al-
ways on her back. I'm certain she was versatile. Sorry, dear.

We're two very dirty old men. Stick out your tongue!

ANN
What is this—

DUDLEY
(*Grabs her wrist, examining her pulse.*)
Stick out your tongue, young lady!
(*She obeys like a child.*)
Had a rather severe cold recently, girl?

ANN
Why yes, but . . .

DUDLEY
You're all right now. Can tell a lot from tongues.

JOHN
There you go, getting vulgar again. You can take a man
out of his mother, but you can't take the mother out of
the man.

DUDLEY
That's just his way of getting back at me. Actually, I loved
my mother very much. She worked my way through college
and medical school, though I didn't find out how until
the day I graduated.

JOHN
Stop putting your business in the street!

DUDLEY
I'm not. It's all in the family. Miss Ann Vanderguild here's
a part of the family, or almost. Ann, here, is your prospec-
tive daughter-in-law, and she'll make a good one too,
Johnny. I stamp her certified.

JOHN
(*To* ANN)
Jeff never wrote us about you.

ANN
Well, he doesn't exactly know I'm here, sir. I mean we never discussed it or anything.

JOHN
Where you from, little lady?

ANN
Canada, sir—I mean, originally I'm from South Africa, sir.

JOHN
This gentleman here is Dudley Stanton. Dr. Dudley Stanton.

ANN
(*To* DUDLEY)
My EKG is excellent too, sir.

DUDLEY
Excellent?

ANN
I mean it's within normal limits, sir. I guess my pulse is very slow, because I used to run track—the fifty-yard dash. I'm a nurse. Perhaps you can help me find a job, sir?

DUDLEY
Oh, these strong black women!

ANN
I'm only strong if my man needs me to be, sir.

JOHN
(*Genuinely elated.*)
You hear that, Dudley, a warrior's woman! A fighter—

DUDLEY
Women always were the real fighters, man, don't you
know that? Men are the artists, philosophers—creating sys-
tems, worlds. Silly dreams and fictions!

JOHN
Fiction is more real, stupid.

DUDLEY
You see, young lady, your prospective father-in-law here is
a philosopher-poet!

JOHN
A poet!

DUDLEY
Philosopher-poet!

JOHN
I'm a poet! A house painter and a poet!

DUDLEY
Then read us one of your masterpieces.

JOHN
Do I have to, Dudley?

DUDLEY
A hundred and ninety bucks' worth—hell yes! You don't
think I come over here to hear your bull, do you? Your
poems, man, by far the better part of you—now read us
one—then give it to me.
(*To* ANN)

You see, I'm collecting them for him, since he doesn't have
enough sense to do it for himself— One day I'm gonna pub-
lish them—

JOHN
Probably under your own name, you goddamn Jew.

DUDLEY
Read us your poem!

JOHN
(*Fumbles through his pants pockets and comes up with
several scraps of paper, which he examines for selection.
He smooths out one piece of paper and begins reading.*)
I am the River Niger—hear my waters—
No, that one ain't right yet.

ANN
Please go on!

JOHN
No, it ain't complete yet. Let's see, yeah, this one's finished.
(*Begins reading from another scrap of paper as lights fade
to a soft amber. A bass jazz theme creeps in.* JOHN *is spot-
lighted.*)
"Lord, I don't feel noways tired."
And my soul seeks not to be flabby.
Peace is a muscleless word,
A vacuum, a hole in space,
An assless anesthesia,
A shadowy phantom,
Never settling anyway— Even in sleep.
In my dreams I struggle; slash and crash and cry,
"Damn you, you wilderness! I will cut my way through!"

And the wilderness shouts back!
"Go around me!"
And I answer,
"Hell, no! The joke's on both of us
And I will have the last laugh."
The wilderness sighs and grows stronger
As I too round out my biceps in this ageless, endless duel.
Hallelujah! Hallelujah! Hallelujah!
I want a muscle-bound spirit,
I say, I want a muscle-bound soul—'cause,
Lord, I don't feel noways tired.
I feel like dancing through the valley of the shadow of
*   death!*
Lord, I don't feel noways tired.

ANN
Beautiful!
(*Bass fades.*)

DUDLEY
(*Takes sheet of paper.*)
This is a blank sheet of paper!

JOHN
I made it up as I went along. Hell, I'll write it down for
you.
(*Holds out his hand insistently for the money.* DUDLEY
counts it out. The doorbell rings suddenly and MATTIE'S
voice is heard—"Mama—John." JOHN *takes the money
eagerly, stuffs it in his pocket, then starts for the door. En
route he stops suddenly, looks at* ANN *as if in a dilemma,
thinks quickly, then crosses to* ANN *and whispers urgently.*)
Look, Ann, if my wife thinks for one minute that you're

trying to get Jeff hooked, she and her crazy mama'll reduce
the whole thing to ashes. Tell 'em you're just passing
through—you and Jeff were friends up there in Canada—
just friends, see—

DUDLEY
Gradually—you've got to ease in gradually. They think
Jeff fell off a Christmas tree or something. No one's good
enough for Jeff— Not even Jeff.

JOHN
Act like a good-natured sleep-in—

ANN
Sleep-in?

DUDLEY
A maid!

MATTIE
Will someone please open the door! I can't get to my key.

GRANDMA
(*At the top of the stairs; she is slightly intoxicated.*)
I'm coming, daughter. I'm coming—
(*Starts humming "Rock of Ages" as she descends the stairs.*)

JOHN
(*To* ANN)
Now remember.
(*Opens door.*)
Hello, Mattie!

MATTIE
The groceries—help me with the groceries.

ANN
Let me give you a hand, Mrs. Williams.
(DUDLEY *gestures to* ANN *approvingly.* MATTIE *takes off her coat, kicks off her shoes, and settles in an easy chair while* ANN *and* JOHN *take the groceries to the kitchen.*)

MATTIE
Who's that young lady?

DUDLEY
A friend of the family.

GRANDMA
How you feeling, daughter? Look a bit peaked to me.

MATTIE
Not too well, Mama; almost fainted on the subway. Was all I could do to get the groceries.

JOHN
(*Coming back.*)
Just need a little soda and water, that's all.

MATTIE
That's what you always say. Something is wrong with me, John. I don't know what, but something's wrong.

DUDLEY
Tomorrow's Saturday. Why don't you come into my office around eleven, let me take a look at you?

MATTIE
No thanks, Dudley. You always manage to scare a person half to death. Have you ever heard of a doctor who ain't got no bedside manner at all, Mama?
(*Laughs.*)

DUDLEY
Well, what do you want—the truth or somebody to hold your hand?

GRANDMA
Both, fool.

MATTIE
Mama!

GRANDMA
Well, he is a fool.

DUDLEY
Well, I guess that's my cue to go home!

JOHN
I'll be damned! Mrs. Wilhemina Brown is going to apologize—

GRANDMA
Over my dead husband's grave—

MATTIE
Mama. You must not feel well yourself.

GRANDMA
I don't, child, I don't. Planned to have your dinner ready, but I been feeling kinda poorly here lately.

JOHN
That's what she always says.

MATTIE
Come to think of it, Mama, your eyes—

GRANDMA
(*Defensively*)
What about my eyes?

MATTIE
Well, they look kinda glassy—

JOHN
(*Knowingly*)
I wonder why?

GRANDMA
(*On her feet.*)
And what in the Lord's name is that supposed to mean?

MATTIE
(*Raising her voice.*)
Will you stop it—all of you.

GRANDMA
(*To* MATTIE)
Are you talking to me? You screaming at your mama?

MATTIE
At everybody, Mama.

GRANDMA
My own daughter, my own flesh and blood, taking a no-good drunk's part against her own mother.

MATTIE
I'm not taking anybody's part. I just want some peace and quiet when I come home. Now I think you owe Dr. Stanton an apology.

GRANDMA
I'll do no such thing.
(*Starts humming "Rock of Ages."*)

MATTIE
I apologize for my mother, Dudley.

DUDLEY
That's okay, Mattie, I wasn't going anywhere anyway.

GRANDMA
I got two more daughters and two manly sons. They'd just
love to have me. Maybe I should go live with Flora.

JOHN
Good idea! Plenty of opportunity to get glassy-eyed over
at Flora's. Yes, indeed.

MATTIE
John, what are you agitating her for?

DUDLEY
. . . Are you afraid, Mattie? To have a checkup, I mean?

MATTIE
(*Pause.*)
Stay for dinner, Dudley.

DUDLEY
Thanks, I will.

ANN
(*At the door.*)
Would you like for me to fix dinner, Mrs. Williams?
(*Pause.*)

MATTIE
Who is this child?

JOHN

Ann Vanderguild. She's from South Africa. She's a friend of Jeff's—just passing through. I asked her to spend the night.

GRANDMA

Where's she going to spend it—the bathroom?

MATTIE

Mama, what's wrong with you tonight?

JOHN

She had a little too much, that's all.

MATTIE

(*To* ANN)

You're welcome, dear. You can stay in Jeff's room tonight. I got it all cleaned up for him. He'll be here tomorrow, you know? Thank the Lord.

ANN

Yes, ma'am! It certainly will be pleasant to see him again.

(MATTIE *looks at* ANN *curiously*.)

I make a very good meat loaf, ma'am. I noticed you've got all the ingredients as I was putting the food away.

MATTIE

You put the food away?

ANN

You seem so bushed.

MATTIE

What a nice thing for you to do. And you read my mind too. Meat loaf is exactly what I was planning to fix. Yes, indeed. Such a pretty girl too.

JOHN
(*To* DUDLEY)
Why don't we make a little run and leave these black
beauties to themselves. To get acquainted—

GRANDMA
Don't be calling me no black nothing. I ain't black! I'm
half-full-blooded Cherokee Indian myself. Black folks is
"hewers of wood and drawers of water" for their masters.
Says so in the Scriptures. I ain't no hewer of no wood my-
self. I'm a Cherokee aristocrat myself.

JOHN
Go on, Grandma, show us your true Cherokee colors, yes,
indeed.

GRANDMA
(*She is obviously inebriated—sings at the top of her voice.*)
Onward, Christian soldiers,
Marching on to war,
With the cross of Jesus
Going on before!
(*Begins shouting as if in church.*)
I'm a soldier myself. I ain't no nigger. A soldier of the
Lord. I ain't no common nigger. So don't you be calling me
no black nothing. Bless my Jesus. Don't know what these
young folks is coming to, calling everybody black!
I'm going home to see my Jesus.
This little light of mine,
Let it shine, let it shine, oh, let it shine. Do Jesus!
(*Shouting gestures.*)

DUDLEY
What I tell you, Johnny. Crabs in a barrel, waiting for a

hand from Canaan land to lift 'em out. Each one shoving and pushing, trying to be first to go. And if Jesus was to put his hand down there, they'd probably think it belonged to just another nigger crab and pinch it off.

JOHN

Ain't that poetic. I can just read the headlines: "Jesus extends his hand to bless his chosen"—'cause we are the chosen, Dudley—"and a hustling dope addict takes out his blade and cuts it off at the wrist."

DUDLEY

For the ring on his little finger. Rub-a-dub-dub, niggers in a tub. Christ extends a helping hand and (JOHN *joins in and they deliver the end of the line in unison*) draws back a nub.

MATTIE

WILL YOU TWO PLEASE STOP IT!
(GRANDMA's *still singing.*)
Mama, why don't you go upstairs and take a rest. Ya'll 'bout to drive me crazy.

GRANDMA

My own daughter treats me like a child. Sending me upstairs. Punishing me 'cause I got the spirit.
(*Starting for the stair. Starts singing once again, but in a more subdued and soulful manner.*)
I know his blood will make me whole.
I know his blood will make me whole.
If I just touch the hem of his garment
I know his blood will make me whole.
(JOHNNY *tries to help her up the stairs.*)
Don't need no help from nobody but Jesus.

(Starts up steps.)
I got Minerva and Flora, and Jacob and Jordan—fine
children. Any one of 'em be tickled pink to have me—
tickled pink! I don't have to stay here.

MATTIE
Mama, go lie down for a while.

GRANDMA
And ain't none of 'em black either. Christian soldiers every
last one of 'em. Mattie's the only black child I ever spawned
—my first and last, thank Jesus.
(GRANDMA *starts up the steps—on the verge of tears.*)
I don't have to stay here—
(Sings.)
I ain't got long,
I ain't got long
To stay here.
Ben Brown was black though. Looked like an eclipse—
sho' nuff. Lord, my God, hallelujah and do Jesus—he was
the ace of spades. And a man, afore God, he was a man—
you hear me, Johnny Williams? My man was a man.
(Exits, humming "Steal Away.")

MATTIE
(*To* ANN)
She gets like that every now and then.

JOHN
More like every other night.

MATTIE
We have a guest, John.

JOHN
Come on, Dudley, let's make that run!

MATTIE
Hold on, Johnny Williams. Where is it?

JOHN
Where's what?

MATTIE
Don't play games, John. This is rent week—remember. Now give it to me.

DUDLEY
All right, great African warrior, do your stuff.

JOHN
Mind your business—

MATTIE
John, I don't feel well. Now, do we have to play your games tonight— Now give it to me.
(JOHN *counts out the money and gives it to her. She counts it rapidly.*)
It's ten dollars short, John.

JOHN
Come on, Mattie. I got to have train fare and cigarettes for the next two weeks.

MATTIE
Stop playing, Johnny. You know if I don't keep it for you, you'll drink it up all at once. Come on, now.
(*He gives her the ten.*)

JOHN

Look, let me have five at least. There's more than enough
for the rent.

(*Pause.*)

Good God, woman, Jeff'll be here tomorrow. Dudley and
I just want to do a little celebrating. Five, woman, hell.

MATTIE

Promise you won't be out late. We got a lot of gettin' ready
to do tomorrow morning.

JOHN

I got this chick, see, sixteen years old, and she is as warm
as gingerbread in the winter time, and we gon' lay up all
night—

MATTIE

We have a young lady here, Johnny.

JOHN

Jeff'll be here by noon. Now, let's see! My little mama just
might let me out of the saddle by noon. Yes, indeed—she
just might!

MATTIE

JOHN!

JOHN

But if I'm not back in time, Jeff'll understand—ain't too
often a man my age gets himself into some young and
tender, oven-ready, sixteen-year-old stuff what can shake
her some tail feathers like the leaves in March.

(*She hands him the five.*)

MATTIE

Get out of here, Johnny Williams.

DUDLEY
Whew! What a warrior—have mercy! You sure do win your battles, man!

JOHN
Oh, shut up! Why fight when you know you're wrong. Let's go!

MATTIE
Dudley—don't let him overdo it. Tomorrow's gonna be a long day.
(JOHN *gets their coats from the hallway*.)

DUDLEY
I'll do my best, Mattie . . .

JOHN
(*Coming back*.)
Don't worry—this black-ass Jew ain't gon' spend enough to even get a buzz—he'll watch over me—just like an old mongrel hound dog I used to own. Damn dog stayed sober all the time—wouldn't even drink beer. He was the squarest, most unhip dog in the world! Come on, monkey chaser, let me tell you 'bout that dog. Named him Shylock!

DUDLEY
Niggers invented name-calling. Mouth, that's all they are, mouth. Good night, ladies. Ann, see you tomorrow.

JOHN
Come on, sickle head. See ya, Ann!

DUDLEY
I'm coming, O great African warrior!
(*They exit*.)

MATTIE

Well, Ann, now you've met the whole family. I hope
Johnny's cussing don't bother you too much.

ANN

No, ma'am! I think he's delightful—he and Dr. Stanton.
My father had a friend like him—always attacking each
other something terrible.

MATTIE

Sometimes they get to going at each other so hard you
think they're gonna come to blows.

ANN

But when they put my father in prison—

MATTIE

In prison—for what?

ANN

They accused him of printing these pamphlets which criti-
cized the government—

MATTIE

Lord, you can't criticize the government over there?

ANN

No, ma'am. Anyway, just after my father was jailed, his
friend just pined away. God—those two men loved each
other.

MATTIE

Men can really love each other, and the funny thing about
it is, don't nobody really know it but them.

ANN

Women don't seem to be able to get along with each other

that way—I mean that deep-loving way. You know what I mean, Mrs. Williams?

MATTIE

Of course I do. It's all 'cause women don't trust one another. Your father? Is he still in prison?

ANN

Yes, ma'am. This is going on his ninth year.

MATTIE

Nine years in prison, my God! How does your mother take it?

ANN

(*Bass melancholy enters.*)
Quietly. Ma takes everything quietly. Dad turned himself in to protect my two brothers. They were the ones operating the press. Dad was just as surprised as the rest of us when the police found the setup in an old chest of drawers in the attic. Before anyone could say a word, Dad was confessing to everything. This dirty old sergeant got mad and hit him in the stomach with his billy club. Dad had a violent temper, but when he got back on his feet, I could see it in his eyes, the decision, I mean. He turned and said, "Boss, if I said something offensive, please forgive an old black fool." And you know what that sergeant did? He hit him again. He hit him again, Mrs. Williams!
(*Overcome with rekindled grief.*)

MATTIE

Oh, I'm sorry, Ann. I must write your mother.

ANN

She'd like that.
(*Pause. She collects herself.*)

My brothers escaped though—stole their way across the border. At first they didn't want to go, they wanted to turn themselves in for Dad, but Ma made 'em go. They live in England now and have families of their own. It wasn't long before the authorities found out that Dad was really innocent, but just because my brothers got away and are free, and just to be plain mean, they kept him in prison anyway. Nine years—nine long years. Those bastards! I despise white people, Mrs. Williams.

MATTIE
Let's talk about something nicer. Tell me about Jeff—(*Bass fades.*)

ANN
Yes, ma'am.

MATTIE
And you—

ANN
Ma'am?

MATTIE
About Jeff and you . . . or you and Jeff.

ANN
I was nursing in Quebec when they brought him into the hospital. He had fractured his ankle skiing. Every time it started paining him, he'd laugh—

MATTIE
He's such a fool.

ANN
Said his dad had taught him to do that. The second night

there were some minor complications and he was in so much pain until the doctor ordered me to give him a shot of morphine. Then he got to talking. Very dreamily at first, like he was drifting in a beautiful haze. He told me all about you and Mr. Williams and Grandma Wilhemina Brown and Dr. Stanton. I almost lost my job—I kept hanging around his room so much, listening to one episode after another.

MATTIE

And that's when you started loving him half to death.

ANN

(*Pause.*)

Yes, ma'am.

MATTIE

That boy sure can talk up a storm. He'll make a fine lawyer. Don't you think so?

ANN

(*Pause.*)

I won't get in his way, Mrs. Williams.

MATTIE

(*After a long pause.*)

No, I don't think you will.

(*Pause.*)

Well, let's see if we can trust each other good enough to make that meat loaf. Why don't you chop the onions while I do the celery?

(*Starts to rise.*)

ANN

(*Stopping her.*)

Oh, no, ma'am, this one's on me.

MATTIE
(*Laughing.*)
I'm very particular, you know.

ANN
I know you are. Jeff's told me a lot about how good your cooking is.

MATTIE
(*Happy to hear it.*)
That boy sure can eat—Lord today. Well, all right, Ann. Let me go on up and get myself comfortable. I'll be right back.
(*She sees the jewelry box on the table—opens it up—takes out a card.*)
What's this?
(*Reads card.*)
"Big-legged woman, keep your dress tail down. Big-legged woman, keep your dress tail down, 'cause you got something under—"

ANN
Go on, Mrs. Williams.

MATTIE
Lord, child, that man of mine.

ANN
Read it, please, ma'am.

MATTIE
"Big-legged woman, keep your dress tail down, 'cause you got something under there to make a bulldog hug a hound."
(*They laugh.*)
Tomorrow's our anniversary, you know.

ANN
Congratulations!

MATTIE
He made this. Can do anything with his hands, or with his head for that matter, when he ain't all filled up on rotgut.
(*Pause.*)
He's killing himself drinking. I guess I'm to blame though.

ANN
Oh, you don't mean that, Mrs. Williams.

MATTIE
It's true.

ANN
But he seems so full of life.

MATTIE
Is it "life" he's full of—or something else?
(MATTIE *exits up the steps.* ANN *busies herself about the kitchen. There is a knock on the front door.*)

MATTIE'S VOICE
Will you get that, please, Ann.

ANN
Yes, ma'am.
(*She crosses and opens the door. A tall, rangy young man in his early twenties rudely pushes his way in. He looks around boldly. He has an air of "I'm a bad nigger" about him.*)

CHIPS
Jeff here?

ANN
(*Sarcastically*)
Come in!

CHIPS
I'm already in. Is Jeff home yet?

ANN
Are you a friend of Jeff's?

CHIPS
Could be. You a friend of Jeff's?

ANN
Yes.

CHIPS
(*Looking her over lewdly.*)
Not bad! As a matter of fact, you look pretty stacked up there.

ANN
Jeff's not home.

CHIPS
Hey, what kinda accent is that? You puttin' on airs or something—
(*She opens the door.*)
Yeah, yeah, I'm going. Tell him Chips came by. Big Mo wants to see him at headquarters as soon as possible. Like it's urgent, ya dig it?

ANN
He won't be here until noon tomorrow.

CHIPS
That's what he wrote the family. He wrote Mo—

ANN
Who's Mo?

CHIPS
(*Laughs.*)
Who's Mo? Mo's the leader.

ANN
The leader of what?

CHIPS
The leader! Wrote Mo he'd be here tonight. Tell him we'll
be back around midnight.
(*Leers at* ANN.)
Yes, sir—just like a brick shithouse.
(*Slaps her on the rear.* ANN *instinctively picks up a heavy
ashtray.*)
Now, don't get rambunctious! If there's anything I can't
stand it's a rambunctious black bitch.

ANN
You get the hell out of here!

CHIPS
(*Takes out a switchblade.*)
Now, what's that ashtray gonna do? If I wanted to, I could
cut your drawers off without touching your petticoat and
take what I want. Now, dig on that?

ANN
Over my dead body.

CHIPS
I made it with a corpse once. Knew a guy that worked in a
funeral home. Pretty chick too—looked something like
you. Wasn't half bad either—once I got into it.

ANN
You damn dog—get out of here!

CHIPS
(*Laughing.*)
Yeah, little fox. I'm going, but I'll be back tonight with
Big Mo.
(*Exits.*)
(ANN *slams the door. She is obviously shaken.* MATTIE
comes down the steps wearing a robe and house slippers.)

MATTIE
Who was that, honey?
(*Sees* ANN's *fear.*)
What happened?

ANN
Some fellow to see Jeff. Called himself Chips.

MATTIE
Chips! That bum! If he or any of them other bums show
up around here again, you call somebody. They're vicious!
Come on, sit down. Catch your breath.

ANN
I'm fine.

MATTIE
Do as I say now!
(ANN *sits.*)
. . . I wonder what they want with Jeff. Jeff used to be
the gang leader around here when he was a teenager. By
the time he got to college, Jeff and his friend Mo had
made the gang decent—you know, doing good things to
help the neighborhood. But I heard lately, the bums gone

back to their old ways. I wonder what they want with Jeff now . . . Well, let's get this. thing ready, and into the oven so we can eat and you can get a good night's rest. You must be exhausted. Bought a new bed for Jeff. You'll sleep like a log.

ANN

Doesn't the couch in the living room let out into a bed, ma'am?

MATTIE

Why, yes.

ANN

Then I'll sleep on the couch. If it's all right with you.

MATTIE

Jeff wouldn't mind a bit you sleeping in his new bed, child! He'll probably say something vulgar about it. Chip off the old block, you know.

ANN

Let it be fresh for him, ma'am, let him christen it with that pretty long frame of his.

MATTIE

(*Laughs.*)
Is he skinny, Ann?

ANN

As a rail.

MATTIE

You're welcome to stay as long as you want. But no tom-foolery between you two, ya understand?

ANN
Oh, no, ma'am.

MATTIE
And another thing. Between you and me and the lamp-post, don't let on to my mother how you feel about Jeff. She don't think nobody's good enough for Jeff. Says he's the spittin' image of my father. Lord, child, she sure loved my father. I'm very lucky in a way, Ann. I come from very loving parents—in their fashion.

ANN
Yes, ma'am, I can see that!

MATTIE
I've often wondered why my sisters turned out to be such hogs.
(*They start on food preparations as lights fade out.*)

(*When the lights come up once more, the house is in dark-ness.* ANN *is asleep on the living-room couch. It is 2 a.m. There is a low rapping at the front door.* ANN *bolts upright. The knocking becomes insistent. Sleepily she answers the door.*)

ANN
Is that you, Mr. Williams?
(*No response.*)
Mr. Williams?
(*No answer. She opens the door.* MO, *an athletic-looking young man in his mid-twenties; his girl friend,* GAIL, *sincere and very much in love with* MO; SKEETER, *who seems constantly out of it and desperate;* AL, *who appears to be intensely observant; and* CHIPS—*all force their way in.*)

CHIPS
Ann—Big Mo. Big Mo—Ann.

MO
Hello, Ann.

CHIPS
Ain't she fine, Mo?

GAIL
Why don't you hush your lips! Simpleton!

MO
(*To* GAIL)
Cool it!
(*To* CHIPS)
Get yourself together, Chips!

AL
Yeah! Get yourself together, nigger. It's past the witching
hour.

MO
(*Ferociously to everybody*)
Ease off! Ease off me!
(*Silent respect.*)
Is Jeff home?

ANN
No!

MO
No! How ya mean—no?

ANN
Just what I said—no!

CHIPS
She's a smarty, Mo.

MO
. . . Okay. You sound like you're for real!

CHIPS
She is, Mo, baby—she is! Let me squeeze up on her a bit.

MO
(*Intensely*)
Shut the fuck up! Excuse me, Ann.
(*To* CHIPS)
And sit down somewhere.
(*To* SKEETER, *falling asleep in the chair*)
You fall asleep—I'm gonna crack your skull, nigger!

SKEETER
Just meditating, chief—just meditating.

MO
(*To* ANN)
Pardon that dumb shit, baby, but, er, we gonna wait right
here till your man shows—all right?

ANN
Look! It is 2 a.m. in the morning. Jeff won't be here
until noon. Now what is it that can't wait till noon?

MO
I can't wait.
(*Pause.*)
Besides—said he'd be here tonight!

ANN
You know what I think? I think you're being very rude—a
bunch of very rude bastards! That's what I think.

CHIPS

Let me squeeze up on her a bit, Big Mo!

(*The conversation is interrupted by the somewhat noisy entrance of* JOHN *and* DUDLEY *through the back door.*)

DUDLEY

That's all you ever do! Blow off at the mouth! Blow off! Blow off! Pardon me, but kiss my brown eye!

JOHN

Looks too much like your face.

DUDLEY

You gimme a royal pain. Give me one for the road, and let me go home.

JOHN

One for the road! Why didn't you buy one for the road before we hit the road. Shylock stingy bastard.

ANN

Mr. Williams! Mr. Williams!

JOHN

(*Coming into the living room—closely followed by* DUD-LEY.)

Yes, Ann—sweet Ann?

(*Sees the crowd.*)

Company, I see.

ANN

Unwanted company, sir.

MO

We're gonna wait for Jeff, Mr. Williams—that's all.

JOHN
Is that Mo—Mo Hayes?

MO
Yes, it is.

JOHN
Well, well, well—I ain't seen you since Skippy was a punk.

MO
I've been around, Mr. Williams.

JOHN
Nice to see you again, son. Who're your friends?

MO
(*Introducing them.*)
Well, sir, this is Gail—my girl. Chips and Skeeter, remember? And Al.

JOHN
Nice to meet you.
(*They exchange greetings.*)
Now go home, gentlemen. It's the wee hours of the morning.

MO
We're gonna wait for Jeff.

GAIL
Let's go, Mo, we can come back later.

JOHN
What'd you say, Li'l Mo? Ain't that your nickname? Li'l Mo? Ain't that what we used to call you?

MO

I said, "We're gonna wait for Jeff."

JOHN

We're planning a celebration for Jeff noon tomorrow, and you're welcome to come—all of you. But that's noon tomorrow.

MO

Can't leave until I see Jeff. Sorry.

JOHN

You're "sorry." You wait until you see how sorry I am when I get back—okay.
(*Exits.*)

GAIL

Mo, baby, let's go. Jeff ain't gon' run nowhere. I mean, what's the hurry?

CHIPS

(*Eyeing* ANN.)
Yeah, what's the hurry?

GAIL

(*Turning on him.*)
You should be in the biggest hurry, nigger, 'cause when Jeff finds out how you been insulting his woman, you're gonna be in a world of trouble.

DUDLEY

Gentlemen, I'd advise you all to leave. Before something presumptuous happens. Can never tell about these black African warrior niggers.

AL
(*Pushing* DUDLEY *into a chair.*)
Shut up.

DUDLEY
(*Blessing himself.*)
Father, forgive them, for they know not what they do.
(JOHN *comes back with an M-1 and a World War II hand grenade.*)

JOHN
(*Highly intoxicated but even more deadly serious because of it.*)
Yeah—well, Father may forgive 'em, but I don't, not worth a damn.

CHIPS
You ain't the only one in here with a smoking machine, man.
(*Opens his coat to reveal a shoulder holster and a revolver.*)

MO
Close your jacket, stupid.

JOHN
Come over here, Ann. Dudley, get your drunk self outta that chair and make it on over here.
(*They follow his instructions. To them*)
I don't know if this old grenade'll work or not, but when I pull the pin and throw it at them niggers, we duck into the kitchen—all right.

AL
This old stud's crazy as shit.

MO
Shut up.

CHIPS
I bet he's faking.
(*Reaches for his revolver.* JOHN *instantly throws the bolt on the M-1. They all freeze for a long moment; finally . . .*)

MO
(*Laughing.*)
You win. You win, Mr. Williams. Dig it? We'll see ya 'round noon. Let's go.
(*They file out.* MO *stops at the door, still laughing.*)
Ya got some real stuff going for you, Mr. Williams.

DUDLEY
Impressive. Presumptuous as hell, but impressive.
(*At this moment* GRANDMA *comes down the steps. She pretends to be sleepwalking. She hums "Rock of Ages" under her breath.*)

JOHN
Shh. The old bag's dreaming.

DUDLEY
What?

JOHN
I've been waiting for this a solid week, Dudley.

DUDLEY
What?

JOHN
Shh. You said you wanted one for the road, didn't you? Then be patient, nigger, be patient.

(GRANDMA *makes her way into the kitchen—seeing no-body. Bass line enters.*)

GRANDMA

Possum ain't nothing but a big rat. I used to say so to Big Ben Brown. "Call it what you want, wife." Always called me wife, you know. "Possum sure got a powerful wild taste to it."

(*She finds her hiding place, pours herself a huge glass of whiskey—talking all the time.*)

That big old black man of mine. Sure could hunt him some possum. Always knew exactly where to find 'em. I sure hated picking out the buckshot though. Sometimes I'd miss one or two, and I'd jes' be eating and all a sudden I chomp down on one. Lordy, that was a hurting thing. Felt like my tooth was gonna split wide open. Sassafras root—and burning pine cones. Do Jesus! Possum's got a wild taste.

(*Bass line fades out.* JOHN *throws his keys into the hall. Startled,* GRANDMA *caps the bottle, hides it, and mumbles her way back up the steps, intermittently humming "Rock of Ages." When she's out of sight,* JOHN *lets out a yelp, gets* GRANDMA's *bottle, and pours each of them a drink.*)

JOHN

Here's to Grandmammy.

(*They drink as* JEFF *enters silently, loaded down with duffel bags and luggage. He sees them, sneaks into hallway without being seen, and hides.*)

Here's to us.

(*Again.*)

Here's to Jeff.

(*Again.*)

Here's to his daddy.
(*Again.*)
Here's to his sweet old mama. Here's to Jesus Christ—one
of the baddest cats to ever drop.
(*They exchange "good nights."* DUDLEY *exits front door.*
JOHN *goes upstairs.* ANN *goes back to sofa—switches off
light. Lights fade to night. Music covers.* JEFF *enters, sees*
ANN *on sofa, and is very pleased. He is a lanky young man
in his middle twenties. There is a heavy seriousness about
him, frosted over with the wildness he has inherited from
his father. His presence is strong and commanding. He is
dressed casually in a turtleneck, bell-bottom slacks, boots,
and long-styled topcoat. Magazines protrude from his over-
coat pocket. His hair is a modified or shortened afro. His
face is clean. He takes off his coat, sits directly opposite*
ANN, *fumbles in his pockets, comes up with a plastic bag
of marijuana, rolls a joint, and lights up. After a couple
of puffs, he leans over and kisses* ANN *on the lips. She
groans; he then takes a heavy drag on the joint and blows
it full in her face. She awakens with a soft sputter. She is
overwhelmed at seeing him. Without saying a word, he
extends the joint to her. She sits upright and drags on it.
He grabs her foot and gently kisses the arch.*)

JEFF
Three whole days—um, um—and I sho' have missed them
big old feet of yours.

ANN
(*Hands him the joint.*)
Are my feet big?

JEFF

Why do you think I always walk behind you in the snow?
You got natural snowshoes, baby.
(*He grabs her roughly but lovingly and kisses her.*)

ANN

I had to come, Jeff.

JEFF

I know. Now, let's get down to the nitty-gritty. How 'bout
some loving, mama?

ANN

Oh, Jeff—I promised your mother.

JEFF

She won't know. And whatcha don't know—
(*Starts taking off his clothes, talking as he does.*)
My dad taught me that where there's a will, there's a way.

ANN

Your dad taught you a lot of things.

JEFF

Yeah. Now we're banging away, right. Oo, ahh, oo, ahh.
And it's sweet—like summer time in December, right?
And just when it really gets good, right? And we're about
to reach the top of the mountain, down the steps comes
Grandma—on one of her frequent sleepwalking things.
And what do I do? I roll over to the wall and drop down
to the other side. Like this—
(*Demonstrates.*)
And nobody knows but us.
(*She kisses him.*)
Daddy Johnny says before a man settles down—which

shouldn't oughta be until he's damn near thirty or more—
(*She kisses him.*)
a young man's mission is the world.

ANN
Well, isn't that what you've been trying to do?
(*She kisses him.*)

JEFF
You keep taking up my time.

ANN
Uh huh.
(*Kisses him as the lights begin to dim. Bass line plays under.*)
You like my feet?

JEFF
Is the Pope Catholic? Can a fish swim? Do black folks have rhythm? Do hound dogs chase rabbits? Your feet got more beauty than sunshine, mama.
(*They kiss as the lights fade to black. Bass line fades.*)

Act Two

Act Two

It is 10:45 the next morning. JOHN, *wearing coveralls made rough with dry paint and a painter's cap, is sweating heavily as he sits pondering his poem. It is obvious that he has suspended the activity of mopping the kitchen floor.*

JOHN
(Bass enters.)
I am the River Niger—hear my waters!
I wriggle and stream and run.
I am totally flexible.
I am the River Niger—hear my waters!
My waters are the first sperm of the world—
When the earth was but a faceless whistling embryo
Life burst from my liquid kernels like popcorn.
Hear my waters—rushing and popping in muffled finger-
            drum staccato.
It is life you hear stretching its limbs in my waters—
(To himself)
Yeah.

(*Quietly he gathers his multiple scraps of paper, folds them neatly, stuffs them into his pocket. Bass fades. He rises to continue mopping the still-half-wet floor. Abruptly he decides to quit and starts for the closet to get his overcoat. He stops as a knock is heard at the kitchen door. He answers it. It is* DUDLEY.)

JOHN
Man, you just in time.

DUDLEY
For what?

JOHN
To make it with me to the Big Apple. The labor's too deep around here for me. Mattie's gon' off her head. Do you know that, I—me—Lightnin' John Williams—more powerful than a speeding locomotive—do you realize that I have mopped this entire house by myself? And now I am making it.

DUDLEY
Without telling the captain?

JOHN
What's that suppose to mean?

DUDLEY
It means that the African warrior is always sneaking around like Brer Rabbit instead of walking up to the captain and saying, "Captain Mattie, I's worked hard 'nuff —I's taking a rest and a mint julep at the Apple!" I mean, I want to see some evidence of your spear-throwing, baby— not just words. Words are outta style.

JOHN
(*Goes to closet in living room. Gets overcoat, comes back, stepping lightly on wet floor.*)
Look, my West Indian corn roaster, I accept the fact that you're a gutless black aristocrat, going thumbs up or thumbs down while your brothers and sisters are being fed to the Lion's Club— So beat your meat while Rome burns —I don't give a piss. Just allow me to paint my own self-portraits—okay, ugly?

DUDLEY
It's pretty chilly out there, man, you better put on a sweater or something, you know.

JOHN
You mean it's pretty chilly for you—that's what I'm trying to tell you. That's you, man, not me!

DUDLEY
Johnny—

JOHN
And don't step on my floor—

DUDLEY
Mattie came over this morning—early. I examined her— and, well, I felt a lot of—irregularities— Anyway—

JOHN
(*Sardonically*)
Well, what're you quacks gonna do now—remove her other tit?

DUDLEY
Johnny.
(*Pause.*)

Maybe even worse. I don't want to alarm her until I'm
sure. I made an appointment for her at Harlem—they'll
do a biopsy—anyway, I'll know as soon as the lab gets
done with it.
(*Pause.*)

JOHN
(*Stricken but defensive.*)
Why you telling me all this if you don't know for sure?
(*Pause.*)

DUDLEY
She came over while you were still asleep—she doesn't
want you to know. I promised I wouldn't tell you.

JOHN
Does she suspect?

DUDLEY
I was very honest with her.

JOHN
That figures! Honesty sticks to some people's mouths like
peanut butter.

DUDLEY
Like you just said, man, I have to deal with things the way
I think best.

MATTIE'S VOICE
(*From upstairs*)
Johnny—Johnny—have you finished the kitchen?

JOHN
She just keeps going, Dudley. I don't know how in hell,
but she keeps on keeping on.
(*Pause.*)

When'll you know for sure?

DUDLEY
By Friday evening.

MATTIE'S VOICE
If you've finished the kitchen, John, how about taking out
those bags of trash.

JOHN
Just keeps on keeping on!
(*Pause.*)

MATTIE'S VOICE
John! Johnny!

JOHN
(*Quietly*)
Johnny's gone to the Apple, you amazing bitch, to cele-
brate an amazing bitch.
(*He and* DUDLEY *exit just as* MATTIE *and* ANN *come down
the steps.*)

MATTIE
(*On the landing, followed by* ANN.)
Ann, I do believe that man's gone! Sneaked out!

ANN
I'll finish, Mrs. Williams.

MATTIE
Ann, thank you so much for your help. I don't think we
coulda finished without you, and that's a fact.
(*Pause.*)
Mama, will you please hurry!

(*To* ANN)
The store will be jam-packed when we get there.

GRANDMA'S VOICE
(*From upstairs*)
If you can't wait for your mother, then go on without me!

MATTIE
Please, Mama!

GRANDMA
Just go on without me, just go on!

MATTIE
(*To* ANN)
There's too much drinking in this house. That's the problem. She's probably hungover.

ANN
Pardon me, Mrs. Williams, but you know about your mother's drinking?

MATTIE
Of course! It's all in her eyes.

ANN
But last night I thought—well—

MATTIE
Child, you got to swallow a lot of truth 'round here to give folks dignity. If Mama knew I knew—I mean really knew I knew—she'd be so embarrassed. Don't you know, I even pretend that John ain't the alcoholic he really is?

ANN
But you're not helping them that way.

MATTIE

Helping them! Who says I ain't? Johnny soon be pushing sixty. He ain't got but a few more years left. If he wants to spend 'em swimming in a fifth a day, who am I to tell him he can't? And Mama, she'll be eighty-three this September. I'm supposed—as the youngsters on my job say— "to blow their cool"? Honey, all we're doing in this life is playing what we ain't. And well, I play anything my folks need me to play.

ANN

I guess that makes sense.

MATTIE

(*Bass enters.*)

That man had two years of college, Ann. Wanted to be a lawyer like Jeff wants to be, you know. He had to stop school because my mother and my two sisters—Flora and Minerva—came up from the South to live with us—for a short time, so they said. Ignorant country girls—they weren't trained to do nothing. I got a job, and together Johnny and I fed 'em, clothed 'em. In a couple of years, John was ready to go back to school, raring to go, don't you know. Then Flora's boy friend came up from good old South Carolina and didn't have a pot to piss in or a window to throw it out of. He and Flora got married, and where do you think they stayed?

(*Yells upstairs.*)

MAMA!

(*Back to* ANN.)

On top of it all, Minerva got herself pregnant by some silly, buck-toothed nineteen-year-old who just vanished. So here comes another mouth to feed— Child, Johnny was

painting houses all morning, working the graveyard shift
at the Post Office, and driving a cab on his days off.
(*Again yells.*)
MAMA PLEASE!
(*Back to* ANN.)
He kept on reading though. And I mean heavy reading.
Smart, Lord knows that man is smart. Student friends of
his were always coming 'round here getting his help in
stuff like trigonometry, organic chemistry, philosophy—
stuff like that—heavy stuff, you know. They used to call
him Solomon. Some of his bummified wino friends still
call him that at the Apple. Solomon!

ANN

Every other word out of Jeff's mouth is "Daddy Johnny
says—"

MATTIE

That's what he did. He poured himself into Jeff. Lord,
had that boy reading Plato and Shakespeare when he was
thirteen years old.
(*Yelling upstairs.*)
I gonna leave without you, Mama.

GRANDMA'S VOICE

I'm a child to be told when to come and go!

MATTIE

You can be too good, Ann. I was actually proud of the way
John worked himself. I read somewhere—in one of John's
psychology magazines—where it's called a Christ fixation,
or something like that.

ANN

But that's kinda nice, isn't it?

MATTIE

Honey, the meek ain't never inherited nothing. No, Ann, if I had to do all over again, I'd do it a whole lot different, believe me. What did we get for it? A chest full of bitterness, that's all. These past few years I've had nothing but bile in my mouth. No, Ann, we got nothing, honey. I mean you'd think they'd call every once in a while.

ANN

My mother used to say, "The giver receives all."

MATTIE

Not in this world, child.

ANN

Somewhere! It must be somewhere—some place—

MATTIE

(*Growing heated.*)

In heaven, honey?

ANN

In a manner of speaking. Treasures—

MATTIE

(*Brooding with anger.*)

In heaven! Treasures in heaven! My man is an alcoholic, the city's trying to condemn this firetrap we ain't even finished paying for yet, and Flora's got a fancy house and a fancy lawnmower upstate. There were times, Ann, times when I wanted John to get mad—really mad—get a bull whip and whip 'em out—just whip 'em right on out. Johnny woulda done it, ya know. Started to several times,

but I'd always manage to cool him down. I got nobody to
blame but myself. ◌

(*Pause.*)

Treasures in heaven—shit. A good man is a treasure. White
folks proclaim that our men are no good and we go 'round
like fools trying to prove them wrong. And I fell right
into the same old dumb trap myself. That's why I can't
get angry with that man no more. Oh, I pretend to be,
but I'm not. Johnny ran a powerful race with a jockey on
his back who weighed a ton. So now he's tired. Do you
hear me? Tired—and he's put himself out to pasture—with
his fifth a day; and I say good for Johnny. I knew he was a
smart man. Good for Johnny.

(*On the verge of tears.*)

If our men are no good, then why are all these little white
girls trying to gobble 'em up faster than they can pee
straight? I rejoice in you young people, Ann. You're the
spring rains we need, 'cause we as a people got a lot of
growing to do. Bless our young folk.

GRANDMA

(*Down the steps.*)

Well, I ain't young like them people you blessing. Them
steps is mighty steep.

(*Bass line fades.*)

ANN

Morning, Mrs. Brown.

GRANDMA

You still here?

MATTIE

Mama, she's here on my invitation. Let's go.

GRANDMA

The gall of a young girl, planting herself right on the boy's doorstep.
(*Crosses to the kitchen.*)

ANN

I'm leaving as soon as Jeff's party's over—

MATTIE

You'll do no such thing. Mama, hush!
(*Embarrassed.*)
Ann, would you kinda give Jeff's room a onceover? I started to do it myself, but for some strange reason the door was locked. Been searching for the key half the morning.
(*Hands* ANN *the key from her apron pocket.*)

ANN

(*Exiting up the stairs.*)
Yes, ma'am.

MATTIE

(*Going to the hall closet, which gives* GRANDMA *a chance to check her bottle in the kitchen.* MATTIE *gets their coats, plus an old creaky shopping cart.*)
Mama, will you stop insulting that child!

GRANDMA

(*Astonished to see empty bottle.*)
That boy needs some time to grow up.

MATTIE

Who's stopping him?

GRANDMA

That audacious girl! That's who.

MATTIE

Mama, she's a nice girl. Besides, Jeff has a mind of his own.

GRANDMA

Ain't no such thing. Not when it comes to a pretty face. And I got a feeling she's animal-natured.

MATTIE

Then you admit she's pretty?

GRANDMA

Well, she's halfway light skin—got good hair. You know what that does to a colored man's mind!

MATTIE

Not today, Mama.
(*Yelling upstairs.*)
Ann, Ann, would you come here a minute.

GRANDMA

Young niggers—old niggers—they all the same! High yellows is still what they want! Young girls these days just like vipers! Anyhow, why you rushing the boy?

MATTIE

I'm not doing a thing, Mama. It's all in your mind.
(ANN *appears at the top of the stairs. She looks like a cyclone has hit her.*)
My God, child, what on earth—is the room that dirty?

ANN

It's a very strong room, ma'am, I can tell you that.

MATTIE

Listen, honey, I got a roast in the oven. Take it out in twenty-five minutes exactly.

ANN
Yes, ma'am.

MATTIE
Come on, Mama.

GRANDMA
(*Ice wind hits her full in the face as* MATTIE *opens the door.*)
Do Jesus!
(MATTIE *and* GRANDMA *exit.* JEFF *appears at the top of the* STAIRS.)

JEFF
How your feets feeling this morning, mama?

ANN
You're insane, you know that—trying to pull my clothes off with your mother right downstairs.

JEFF
Hey, ain't I got a groovy mama?

ANN
She's wonderful.

JEFF
You ever look at her feet? She's got some boss dogs—

ANN
Jeff, I'm moving into a hotel this evening—your grandma's a little too much—even for me.

JEFF
Look, today's my homecoming and tomorrow's Sunday—a day of rest. Monday we'll find you a place—okay? Now,

why don't you cool your heels and let's get a quickie be-
fore the inmates return—
(*Pause.*)
Don't worry! Dad won't be back for at least an hour and
Mama always gets carried away shopping—
(*Knock on the front door.*)
And you will not be saved by the bell. See who it is.
(*She goes to peephole in door.*)

ANN
It's Mo's friend—Skeeter, and I believe the other one's
called Al.

JEFF
Skeeter! Send them away! No! That wouldn't be cool.
That means Mo's not far behind. Let them in! Tell them
to make themselves comfortable, that you've got some last-
minute cleaning to do upstairs, and come on up. For all
they know, I'm not here yet.

ANN
As simple as that, huh?

JEFF
Right!
(*Another knock.*)

ANN
You're crazy.

JEFF
(*Starts upstairs.*)
Can I help it if I'm in heat for your feet?
(*Exits.* ANN *answers the door.*)

SKEETER

Hey, we come for the party. Mo wanted us to break in early so's we could rap a taste before Jeff's folks gits into him, ya dig.

ANN

Come on in. Skeeter, isn't it?

SKEETER

Ain't it.

ANN

And Al?
(AL *nods. They enter.* SKEETER *is jittery. It is obvious he is in heavy need of a fix, but he's clever enough to hide the chilling cold running through him.*)
Can I take your coat?
(AL *gives her his coat.*)
What about you?

SKEETER

That's okay—I mean, I'm cool.

ANN

Can I get you a beer or something?

AL

Not right now, thanks.

ANN

Skeeter?

SKEETER

I'm cool, sister, I'm cool. Is Jeff here?

ANN
Not yet.
(*There is a pounding from upstairs.*)

SKEETER
What's that?

ANN
Please make yourselves comfortable. Jeff's due shortly, and
I've got to get his room cleaned up a bit.
(*Starts up the stairs.*)
There's beer and stuff in the refrig. Just call if you need
me.

SKEETER
Yeah. Everything's everything.
(ANN *exits.*)
I hate smart-ass black bitches.
(*Lights a cigarette.*)

AL
So do I, sweet baby.

SKEETER
Stop being so obvious. If Mo ever finds out about your
sweet shit—

AL
He won't, sweet baby.

SKEETER
Don't give me that sweet-baby jive. Have you got it?

AL
Well, fuck you. I hate smart-ass dope fiends.

SKEETER
Aw, come on, Al, don't catch an attitude.

AL
I'll catch a 'tude if I so desire. I got the shit and you want it, so walk soft or go to Phoenix House, nigger man.

SKEETER
(*Shivering.*)
Come on, man. I'm sorry.

AL
You sure is. You the sorriest motherfucker I ever run across.

SKEETER
Come on, man. Mo'll be here in a minute.

AL
Finish telling me 'bout Buckley.

SKEETER
Gimme the stuff first.

AL
I want to know 'bout Buckley.

SKEETER
(*Shivering.*)
I'm cold, man—cold.

AL
Then talk to me, sugar baby.

SKEETER
What you want to know?

AL

Who ripped him off?

SKEETER

Why you so anxious to know?

AL

Those motherfuckers in Queens claim they did it. They always claiming credit for what we do.

SKEETER

We? You weren't even heard of when it happened.

AL

Well, it's we now, ain't it? Had to be you, Chips, or Mo!

SKEETER

Why's that?

AL

Well, I know you cats wouldn't trust none of the young bloods in the organization to do an important job like that.

SKEETER

Why you want to know 'bout Buckley? You sure you from the home office, nigger? Ever since they sent you here, you been bugging me 'bout Buckley!

AL

Look, I fight for niggers, 'cause I hate the devil pig—but I don't trust niggers as far as I can spit. If there's a finger man on the team, I want to know who it is. Somebody might make a mistake and put him on my ass. You sure get heated up 'bout simple party gossip. So heated up, sugar baby, you clean forget all 'bout that deep-freeze chill

slipping and sliding through your bones. You even bite the hand that lights your fire, don't you, sugar baby?
(*In furious desperation,* SKEETER *suddenly reaches inside his coat, but* AL *is too quick. At about the same time they both produce their revolvers.*)
Don't make the mistake of thinking a sissy can't play that Gary Cooper shit if he want to, nigger man.
(*They face each other.*)

SKEETER
(*Seething.*)
I hate your guts.

AL
All that's cool. But I got what it takes to get your guts together, and don't you forget it. I can draw a gun like Sammy Davis, and I was a Golden Gloves champion two years in a row. I got all the hole cards, baby. I could even pull the trigger faster than you right now, 'cause I stays in shape, baby, and you is a dope fiend.
(SKEETER *puts his gun away.* AL *follows suit.* SKEETER *paces about the room, clutching his stomach as* AL *watches, underneath enjoying* SKEETER's *pain. Finally,* SKEETER *turns to* AL, *pleading in anguish.*)

SKEETER
Give me the shit, Al.

AL
I had it for you all the time. You just been running backward and now you're facing the right way, that's all, sugar baby. Just answer me one teeny-tiny little question. Was it you?

SKEETER
No.

AL
Chips?

SKEETER
(*Almost screaming.*)
It was an outside dude.

AL
Who?

SKEETER
(*He clutches his stomach.*)
He wouldn't give his name. He just did it and split. Last
I heard he was in Frisco.
(*Satisfied,* AL *searches his pockets. Unknown to* AL, SKEETER
suppresses a chuckle.)

AL
(*Handing him a package of wrapped tin foil.*)
Here, snort on this. It oughta hold you till after the meet-
ing. It's strong as a horse's ass.
(*Using the tip of his little finger,* SKEETER *snorts greedily—
first one nostril, then the next.*)
Later on we can really take care of business.
(*Watches* SKEETER *awhile.*)
Why'd ya'll hate Buckley so?

SKEETER
(*Calming down rapidly.*)
He was on the narco squad. Useta raid and steal scag and
push it to the school kids. Always little girls. He'd get 'em

hooked, strung out, then make em do freakish shit for a fix. Any one of us woulda blown him away. ⟍
(*Pause.*)
Hey, I seen you trying to feel up on Chips's little brother.

AL
(*Excitedly*)
You lie, nigger.

SKEETER
If you'd make it with Chips, you'd make it with anybody. Don't give me that funny look, nigger.

AL
You lie!

SKEETER
If I tell Mo 'bout it, he'll bust both of you mothers. Ain't that some shit. And you mean to tell me you don't know 'bout Chips? He stuck his joint in an embalmed cunt. And he brags about it! You know what Mo calls him when he really gets mad at him? Femaldehyde Dick.
(*Laughs.*)

AL
That shit you just snorted ain't gon' last forever, you know.

SKEETER
Oughta call you Femaldehyde Brown Eye.

AL
Ya never miss the water till the well runs dry.

SKEETER
Don't give me that shit. We got a working relationship— the three of us.

AL
What three?

SKEETER
You, me, and Chips. You give me scag 'cause you know I know where you at— I don't tell Mo where you at 'cause I need the scag. Chips don't tell him 'cause he digs fags. That's where he's at! Now, you keep your eye—your brown eye—on that relationship 'cause all three of us is walking on the same razor blade, sugar baby, and don't you forget it, 'cause our asses could get cut in half!
(*Laughs uproariously. There is a knock on the door.*)

AL
Answer the door, dope fiend!
(SKEETER *goes to the door, peeks through.*)

SKEETER
It's Femaldehyde himself.

AL
Flake off, nigger—I'm warning you!

SKEETER
You want to know something else, Alfreida? That shit about an outside man ripping off Buckley—I made that up.

AL
Your ass is gon' be mine. Wait and see!

SKEETER
(*Laughing.*)
You wanta know something else? I'm supposed to pick up

some good stuff as soon as we finish rapping with Jeff. I
don't really need your shit.
(*Laughs and opens the door.*)

CHIPS
(*To* AL)
What's this clown laughing about?

SKEETER
(*Holding his sides.*)
Gary Cooper here just got some lemon in his sucker—
(*Laughs. The front door is left slightly ajar.*)

CHIPS
Dig these happenings. A young dude who said he was from
the *Times* was hanging around headquarters all morning,
asking questions about you know who.

SKEETER
Buckley!

CHIPS
Dig it!

SKEETER
(*Eyeing* AL.)
Ain't that interesting!
(*Laughs.*)

CHIPS
The pigs is restless. So you cats be careful.
(ANN *appears at top of stairs.*)
Well, bless my soul—if it ain't foxy mama. How 'bout a
hug and a squeeze, foxy mama?
(*To* SKEETER)
Who else is here?

SKEETER
Just us chickens.

CHIPS
You mean foxy mama is by her little old self—in this big
house?

ANN
(*Trying to ignore him.*)
Jeff'll be here in a minute, everybody.

CHIPS
Then we got to git it before he gets here, right, mama?
All I want you to do is show me the upstairs.
(CHIPS *starts up the steps after her.*)

ANN
What are you trying to prove?

AL
Chips—

SKEETER
Man, can't you act civilized?

CHIPS
Mind ya business.

SKEETER
Chips—come on, man.

ANN
It's all right—he wants to see upstairs— I'll show him.

CHIPS
(*Swats her on her rear.*)
Now you talking, foxy mama. All I wants is a hug and a

squeeze. You dudes take it easy now. And call me when you see Mo coming.
(ANN *hesitates, and he shoves her ahead of him.*)
He who hesitates is lost, mama.
(*They exit upstairs.*)

AL

Some niggers ain't got no couth—

SKEETER

There goes Femaldehyde!
(*In the next moment we hear a loud yell from* JEFF *and much commotion. A second later* JEFF *comes down the stairs with* CHIPS's *revolver pressed against* CHIPS's *head.* ANN *brings up the rear.*)
Here comes Femaldehyde!

CHIPS

Come on, Jeff, man, I was only fooling, man. I mean, you know me, Jeff. I didn't know she was your woman, man. Honest!
(JEFF *smacks him brutally across the face.*)

SKEETER

Lighten up, Jeff.

AL

Yeah, like you made your point, man.
(JEFF *turns and looks at them, saying nothing. The ferocity of his stare silences them.*)

ANN

Jeff—it's okay.
(JEFF *wallops* CHIPS *in the pit of his stomach.* CHIPS's *knees buckle to the floor.*)

CHIPS
It's your world, baby! It's your world!

ANN
He's not worth it, Jeff. Please, baby, for me—okay?
(MO *and* GAIL *enter, almost unseen.*)

CHIPS
I was only fooling, Jeff. Honest.

JEFF
Fooling with a gun at my woman's head?

CHIPS
I wouldn't hurt ya woman, man. It ain't even loaded.

JEFF
(*Places gun against* CHIPS's *temple.*)
So if I pull the trigger, it won't matter.
(*Cocks hammer.*)

CHIPS
(*Hysterical.*)
Oh shit—oh shit— Don't do that, Jeff. Please don't do
that.

JEFF
The next time I catch you looking cross-eyed at my woman,
I'm gonna rid the world of one more jive-ass nigger. Now,
get out of here.

MO
Let him stay, Jeff. As a favor to me.

JEFF
(*Turns to see* MO.)
I despise irresponsible niggers, Mo.

MO

I'll be responsible for him.

JEFF

Then he'd better become shy, quiet, and unassuming.
'Cause that's the only kind of nigger I tolerate in my house.

MO

Well, you sound like the Jeff I used to know back when.

GAIL
(*To* CHIPS)
You act more like a pig than the pigs.

MO

Old Femaldehyde!

SKEETER
(*Laughing.*)
Rides again.

MO
(*Referring to the revolver.*)
Is that your steel, man?

SKEETER

It's Chips's.
(*Laughs.*)

MO
(*Collaring* CHIPS *angrily.*)
What! Not only do you insult a personal friend of mine—
but you let him take your steel! That's unforgivable, cluck.
You better get it back or another one just like it—posthaste

—you dig me. Loss of a weapon is a crime against the organization. Do you dig them apples, Femaldehyde?
(SKEETER *holds his sides laughing.*)
(*To* SKEETER)
Shut up!

GAIL
(*Extends her hand to a still angry* JEFF.)
I'm Gail.

JEFF
Hi!

MO
This is my woman, Jeff. And of course you know Skeeter—

JEFF
Hey, Skeets.

SKEETER
(*Shaking* JEFF's *hand.*)
What's happening, big Jeff?

MO
And Al here I wrote you 'bout.
(*They shake hands.*)
Now, can we all settle down awhile and rap?
(*Everybody finds a comfortable spot, and there is an uneasy silence.*)

ANN
Who wants a beer?
(*Everybody nods.*)

MO

Why don't you help her, Gail?

GAIL

Sure.

(ANN *and* GAIL *cross the room to the kitchen.*)

MO

Now, dig this, Brother Jeff. What I'm about to run down to you is only to make a point, and stop being so pissed. Everybody's edgy.

JEFF

I'm not edgy, baby, I'm about to draw blood.

CHIPS

Look, man, I'm sorry—okay.

JEFF

Negative, baby—not okay, not okay worth a damn.

MO

Jeff—Jeff—why do you think Chips had the nerve to shoot on your woman like he did? I think it's because of your letters, man!

JEFF

You showed *them* my personal letters to you?!

MO

Yeah! And you know why? 'Cause they sounded like you were turning, man, dig it—turning into a weak, halfway-in-between, neither here nor there Oreo cookie. I mean, the last thing we expected was Big Brother, bad-ass Jeff, our main man who we been waiting to welcome back to the trenches suddenly deciding to go trip off to law school,

rapping 'bout the Constitution and a whole lot of the
upside of the wall shit . . . Jeff, remember the time I
had to fight Billy Richardson? Remember how his brothers
kept clipping me and pushing on me every time it looked
like I was winning? Remember that shit?

JEFF
What's the point?

MO
It was suppose to be a fair fight to see who was to gain
control over St. Nicholas Avenue, right? I mean we par-
layed and parlayed, and it was agreed upon—we had a
verbal contract. And what they do? Billy's older brothers
held you against the fence while he and the younger punks
in his gang went to work on me. I was ready to give up,
man, I mean all the wind was outta my sail, baby. And I
looked up, and there you were, crying, baby, crying—trying
to break loose from cats twice your size, can you dig it? Try-
ing to break loose to help your main man, your brother,
and crying, and somehow your shit got into me, and I beat
Billy until he was screaming for mercy—his own boys let
up when they dug what was happening!

Well, a dumb-ass nigger and a pig are one and the same!
They don't understand agreements and contracts; they're
beasts—the only thing a beast understands is guts and
determination. We ran the whole goddamn neighborhood
after that, and we had one motto, "Keep on keeping on!"
And anybody who gave up in a fight got his ass kicked
when he got back to the club.

All that shit about legal pressure, the democratic process
bullshit. I tell you, man, the law ain't never helped the
black man do nothing. The law is the will of the prevailing

force, which is the pig in this country—and you want to be a lawyer? That Constitution ain't nothing but bullshit, don't you know that yet, man?

JEFF

Make it work and you've got a formidable weapon.

MO

I say, burn the motherfucker! Look, man, we've gone all those routes. We've petitioned, we've sat in, shitted in, demonstrated until we got fallen arches, etc., etc., etc., and where did it get us, huh? Things are worse! Contracts!? I'm talking 'bout revolution, man.

JEFF

That word's been talked to death. The revolution ain't nothing but talk, talk, talk, and I ain't gonna waste my life on talk. Niggers are jiving, man, can't you see it? That's all I heard from the black troops in the air force—revolution. Where's the gun factory, the bomb-assembly plant? We're shucking and jiving, man—that's all. Law is something concrete, something I can *do*, not talk about.

MO

To a certain extent, you're right, Brother Jeff. Black people have been shucking and jivin', passing the buck. Well, we are the buck-ending committee. We ain't just talking, baby. We proving it. And in a few days we gonna serve notice on whitey that the shit has only begun to hit the fan. We want you with us, man.

JEFF

You've got it all figured out, Mo. You don't need me.

MO

We don't need nothing, baby, we just *want* you with us.

JEFF

Maybe I'm out of it, Mo. Maybe I don't know what's really happening any more. Yes, I'm still for whatever advances the cause of black folks, but I reserve the right to choose my own weapons. I don't have to fight with yours, Mo, and I respect your right not to have to fight with mine . . . All I know is that right now my convictions rest elsewhere . . . Now, gentlemen, my folks will be making it back pretty soon and I'd like the atmosphere to change into something a little bit more groovy, ya dig?

MO

Yes, sir, Lieutenant Williams, sir.

JEFF

Or *leave*.

MO

Is that an order, sir?

JEFF

You're in my house, nigger.

MO

I don't play that word, man. You throw it 'round a little too much.

JEFF

Oh yeah, well, you pat your foot while I play it, nigger.

MO

You either gon' be with us or against us, Brother Jeff. Nobody stays uncommitted in this neighborhood. Besides, we can make you do anything we want you to do.

JEFF
How you gonna do that, brother?

MO
Every time you poke your head out your door, you can be greeted with rocks, broken glass, garbage bags, or doo-do. And if that don't work . .
(ANN *and* GAIL *return from kitchen.*)
And if that don't work . . .

JEFF
(*Furious.*)
If that don't work, what?

MO
We can work on your moms and pops. They might come home and find the whole house empty, no furniture or nothing, motherfucker.

JEFF
Oh no, baby, you're the motherfucker. You really are the motherfucker!
(*Controlling his fury at* MO.)
You jive-ass nigger. Mr. Zero trying to be Malcolm X. List' old world, list' to *the* revolutionary. See him standing there with his Captain America uniform on. Look at his generals. Skeeter the dope head and Chips the sex pervert. Mo the magnificent, playing cops and robbers in his middle twenties, trying to be somebody and don't know how. The one advantage I have over you, Mo, is my daddy

taught me to see through my own bullshit, to believe that
I don't need bullshit to be somebody. Go back to school,
Mo, you're smart enough.

GAIL
Don't talk to him like that!

MO
You been thinking this shit for a long time, ain't you,
nigger?

JEFF
Affirmative. And if you try any shit on my folks, your ass
is mine, nigger. Or have you forgotten what a mean, evil,
black bastard I can be, how you could whip everybody in
the neighborhood and how I could whip the piss out of
you, how I got more determination in my little toenail
than you got in your whole soul, nigger!

MO
At least you still talk bad.

JEFF
I ain't bad. I'm crazy, motherfucker. Now you, your dope
fiend, and Marquis de Sade, get the fuck outta here, and
don't call me—I'll call you.

MO
(*Not too frightened but impressed.*)
Let's go. This ain't the end, Jeff. I suggest you think about
what I said and think hard.

JEFF
Just make it, man. And remember
(*Places gun to* CHIPS's *temple.*)
I'm fully armed, thanks to General Chips here.

MO

Don't make fun of me, Jeff.

JEFF

Why should I do that, you're a self-made comedian.

CHIPS

I think we should—

MO

You ain't had a thought in your life, cluck.
(*They all exit.*)

JEFF

(*Walking around the room.*)
Goddamn, goddamn! . . . Where's the hootch? I know
Pop got some somewhere.
(*Looks around frantically.*)
I know the refrig used to be one of his favorite places.
(*Finds it.*)
Damn! Almost half full! Lawd hep me! 'Cause these nig-
gers don' gon' crazy.
(*Takes a drink.*)
Hep me, Lawd. Hep me, hep me, Lawd.
(*Takes another drink and sings the words . . .*)
" 'Cause the niggers don' gon' crazy!"

ANN

That's enough.

JEFF

Ann, my love, the most glorious bitch I ever don' run
across—let's get married. Let's get married and screw right
at the ceremony. Monday we'll get the license. There's a
three-day wait—Tuesday, Wednesday, and Thursday—

Friday we'll get high off this bad-ass smoke I been saving
and fly on to the preacher.

ANN
Are you serious?

JEFF
Indubitably.

ANN
Oh, Jeff, why so sudden?

JEFF
Honey, with the way these niggers is acting up 'round
here, I figure I better get me some hep.

ANN
Jeff, I—

JEFF
I know you love me to pieces, and I don't blame you one
bit.

ANN
You conceited—

JEFF
The problem is, I don't really love you.
(*Pause.*)
I glory for you, baby. Besides, you got the bossest dogs I
ever seen.
(*They kiss and embrace. There's a knock at the door. It's*
GAIL.)

GAIL
Can I come in?

ANN
Of course.
(ANN *brings her into the kitchen.*)

GAIL
Mo thinks I stopped at the store to get cigarettes.

ANN
Would you like a drink?

GAIL
No, I don't drink.

ANN
Relax, Gail.

GAIL
Jeff, when I was a little girl, all I used to do was watch you and Mo running everything, the whole neighborhood together, always cool—no strain, ya know what I mean? You two cats were so beautiful together . . . Maybe it was wrong for Mo to come down on you so hard tonight, Jeff, after three years—but you the only person he trusts, Jeff. Writing to you the years you were away was his way of forgetting you had ever left. Now he needs you more than ever, Jeff. The organization has gotten to be a real hassle.

JEFF
How could it be anything else with those nothings he's got at his back? I mean, it's hard to be out front when you got shit at your back.

GAIL
That's why he needs you bad, Jeff. Mo only looks at the good in people. Skeeter and Chips been with you cats ever

since you started gang-bopping. Mo's not dumb, he knows
their hang-ups. But they swore to him they'd stay clean.
Anyway, when you trying to build an army outta people
who been buried in garbage all their lives, you can't expect
they gon' all of a sudden start smelling like roses. In time,
Mo believes, the movement will straighten 'em out for
good.

JEFF

Mo's a saint. I'm a realist.

GAIL

Then help him, Jeff, help him.

JEFF

It's not just those okeydoke creeps 'round him, Gail. We
don't see eye to eye. Mo thinks he's still back in the old
days, leading a gang. Times have changed.

GAIL

You could influence him, Jeff.

JEFF

He doesn't need me, Gail. He's sure about where he's go-
ing and confident about how to get there—

GAIL

That's not true, Jeff.

JEFF

And all that bull about threatening me and my folks—I'd
jump in an elephant's chest behind that jive.

GAIL

He was only saying that for them—

JEFF
Why crucify me for a bunch of nothings, baby?

GAIL
Do you know Mo, Jeff?

JEFF
I thought I did.

GAIL
If you really know him, Jeff, then you know he didn't mean what he said. He's desperate, Jeff. Things are all mixed up. A few years ago, everything was straight up and down—simple—*right on for the people*. Now everything's falling apart, splitting up, people going every which way. And Mo's gotten into some heavy, scary things, Jeff. Right now the heat's on 'cause a pig cop was wasted a few months ago. And this Friday Mo plans to destroy a new state office building going up, or else mess with one of the police stations.
    You think he's so cocksure? Well, he ain't. He don't even know if what he's doing is right any more. I know—'cause I see him get up in the middle of the night and stare out the window and talk to himself—talk to his demons. Don't let his tough act fool you, Jeff. Behind his real together front, he's about to snap. You hear me, Jeff, he's gonna snap. I know it. Lord God, help him, Jeff Williams. Even if you don't see eye to eye with him, find a way to help him. The hell with the movement, help HIM! Help him, please, before he breaks apart. Help him, Jeff.
(*She sobs uncontrollably.* ANN *comforts her.*)

ANN
He will, Gail, he will—I know he will.

(*To* JEFF)
I like him, Jeff. His approach may be all wrong, but he's
fighting. He's honest and he's fighting. He's a determined
black man, just like you, Jeff.

JEFF
All right. I'll try, Gail, I'll try. I promise you.
(*The front door swings open. It's* MATTIE *and* GRANDMA,
GRANDMA *pushing a shopping cart,* MATTIE *loaded down
with grocery bags. Bass line enters.*)

MATTIE
Lawdamercy. The door's wide open!

GRANDMA
That hussy girl's doings!
(MATTIE *sees* JEFF.)

MATTIE
Lawdamercy! Lawdamercy! Jeff!
(*She rushes to embrace him.*)
You big old good-for-nothing thing.
(GRANDMA *starts for him.*)

GRANDMA
Ben Brown! The spitting image of Ben Brown. Ben Brown
all over again.
(*She embraces him.*)
Ain't black like Ben Brown, but he sho' do carve himself
out a fine figure, don't he, Mattie?

JEFF
(*Eyeing her lewdly.*)
You don't do so bad yourself, sweet meat!

GRANDMA
You ought to be ashamed of yourself.
(*Hugs him once more.*)

MATTIE
You weren't supposed to be here till noon.

JEFF
I'll go back and come at noon.

MATTIE
Go on, boy, stop acting so simple.

JEFF
Can't help it, Mama. I got my two foxes back again—Cleopatra—
(*Referring to* GRANDMA.)
and her sidekick.
(*Referring to his mother.*)

MATTIE
I'll sidekick you.

JEFF
(*Hugging them both at the same time.*)
Got my two womens back again.

MATTIE
Stop being so rough with your simple self. What they been feeding you—bread and water? You too thin to say grace over.

JEFF
Know what I wants for dinner? Some corn bread, yeah. And some of Grandma's mustard greens, Mama.

GRANDMA
(*Salutes him.*)
Yes, sir.

JEFF
And black-eyed peas. And some of your candied sweets,
Grandma, with lemon and raisins all over 'em, yeah!

GRANDMA
And roast beef!

JEFF
Do Jesus, and bless my soul, Grandma Brown! And don't
forget the lemonade.

GRANDMA
A gallon of it. Made it myself.

JEFF
And some sassafras tea.

GRANDMA
Got it fresh from that new health-food store.
(*Pause.*)

JEFF
Ma, do you realize that I'm home for good—

MATTIE
Thank God!

JEFF
No more okeydoke. No more time outta my race against
time. No more stuff, messing with my mind. I'm me—Jeff
Williams, because Daddy Johnny named me—before ya'll
claimed me on your income tax! And ya'll sho' is looking
gooooooooood—good God, good!

MATTIE
Go on, boy!

JEFF
Mama, this is Gail. Mo Hayes's girl friend.

MATTIE
Nice to know you, Gail.

GAIL
(*Extending her hand.*)
Heard a lot about you, Mrs. Williams.

JEFF
And this is my grandma, Gail. Grandma Wilhemina Geneva Brown.

GRANDMA
There you go, acting the fool, Jeff Williams. You know I can't stand "Geneva."

GAIL
My pleasure, Mrs. Brown.

GRANDMA
What? Oh, yes. How do, child.

JEFF
And this is Ann!

GRANDMA
(*Disapprovingly*)
We've met.

MATTIE
The best—of—friends!
(GRANDMA *grunts.*)

JEFF
(*Ignoring* GRANDMA.)
Well, I'm glad 'cause this foxy mama here and your son—
me—the baddest dude to catch an attitude—God's gift to
the female race—"for God so loved the world that he
gave—"

MATTIE
I'll take off my shoe and knock holes in your head, boy!

JEFF
Mama, what I'm trying to tell you—

GRANDMA
You gon' marry this here brazen gal?
(*Bass fades.*)

MATTIE
Mama!

JEFF
Indubitably!

GAIL
That's beautiful! Just beautiful!

GRANDMA
Do Jesus, Uncle Sam don' took my child—

MATTIE
Your child—

GRANDMA
And turned him into a cockeyed ignoramus.

MATTIE
Don't pay any attention to her, Ann.

ANN
Jeff, I think I'll walk to the corner with Gail.

JEFF
You will not!

GRANDMA
You too young to fart good—talking 'bout getting married.

JEFF
I'm twenty-five!

GRANDMA
Stop lying! You ain't outta your teens.

JEFF
I was twenty-two when I left, Grandma.

GRANDMA
(*To* MATTIE)
Lawd, Mattie, is my child don' got that old on me?

MATTIE
Your *grandson* is that old, Mama.

GRANDMA
Do Jesus! Time sho' do fly, don't it? 'Tweren't yesterday I
was getting myself all sprayed up changing your diapers.

JEFF
(*Slowly, deliberately*)
That was twenty-five years ago, Grandma.

GRANDMA
(*Coming out of her reveries.*)
Don't make no difference. You're too young to get your-

self saddled with a wife. Next thing you know, here comes one crumbsnatcher—then two—

JEFF
Then three—then four. It's pretty lonely not having any brothers and sisters, I can tell you.

GRANDMA
A lodestone! A lodestone 'round your neck, a-dragging you down.

MATTIE
What about law school, Jeff?

JEFF
Oh, we gon' do that too. I mean them crumbsnatchers ain't coming until we are ready for 'em. Ann's gonna use the loop, birth-control pills, the rhythm method, and the diaphragm, and Emko!

GRANDMA
There sure is a whole lot Emko babies walking 'round here.

MATTIE
(*To* JEFF)
Well, you certainly seem to know an awful lot 'bout it.

JEFF
Like I said before, I'm *twenty-five.* Be twenty-six the twenty-fourth of this month, Mama.

MATTIE
You still don't have to know so much in front of your mother.

JEFF
I apologize.

GRANDMA
(*Blurting out a long-pent-up reality.*)
Look at your father. He wanted to be a lawyer, didn't he?
Then I jumped on his back, then them two no good daughters of mine, then their two empty-headed husbands—then
you. The load was so heavy till he couldn't move no more.
He just had to stand there, holding it up.

MATTIE
(*Very serious.*)
Then you know about it?

GRANDMA
What do you think I am? A sickle-headed, lopsided, cock-
eyed ignoramus like your son here?

MATTIE
Oh, so you admit he's my son?

GRANDMA
He's your son, but he's my child.

MATTIE
(*Turning to* ANN.)
Have ya'll given it serious thought, Ann?

ANN
He just asked me, Mrs. Williams.

GRANDMA
Is that all you gon' do? Talk? You gon' let this brazen
hussy just take my child away?

MATTIE

Mama, why don't you go to your room and cool off a bit.

GRANDMA

She is brazen. Camping right on his doorstep. I call that bold, brash, and brazen! And conniving too! A pretty face'll sho' kill a man—even a good man.

(*To* ANN)

And not even mean to! You gon' take that on your shoulders, child, you gon' kill your man before he can stand up good yet? Is that what you gon' do? I did it. Mattie did it. She let me help her do it.

MATTIE

Mama!

GRANDMA

Don't mama me. Where's my medicine? I don't want to be here and watch my child leap into deep water. Lawda-mercy, no! Where is my medicine? Where's my pocket-book?

JEFF

(*To* MATTIE)

Is Grandma sick, Ma?

MATTIE

In a manner of speaking.

(GRANDMA *finds her purse. There is a large bulge in it. She seems satisfied. She starts up the stairs, singing "Rock of Ages."*)

GRANDMA

Hep him, Lawd! Hep my child!

(*She exits, singing.*)

JEFF
(*To* ANN)
Is this what you've been putting up with?

MATTIE
Ann's a fine girl, Jeff. You know I believe that, don't you, Ann?

ANN
Thank you, Mrs. Williams.

MATTIE
And you know women get silly over their sons and, well, grandsons.

ANN
Yes, ma'am.

MATTIE
My personal opinion—if ya'll are interested—is that you should wait awhile—at least until Jeff's finished law school.

JEFF
Ever since I got home, people been telling me what to do and what not to do. You talking about a lodestone—that's the heaviest lodestone in the world . . . I want to marry Ann 'cause she is a fine girl, Mama. Something rare— came home and found my sweet baby here—it was like God was saying, "This is your woman, son. I can't let you do nothing that dumb. I can't let you leave her. I made her for you!" And goddamn it—

MATTIE
Jeff!

JEFF

I'm following what I hear inside my soul!

MATTIE

(*Pauses for a long moment, finally embracing him strongly, on the verge of tears.*)

Then you do that, baby. You follow the Lord. As mad as He makes me sometimes, I don't think He's ever really told me wrong.

(*Hugs* ANN *lovingly.*)

Come on in here and help me fix this food, girl. You're one of the family now. I guess I knew you were the moment I laid eyes on you.

(*To* JEFF)

Why do you like to shock people so? You know how your grandmother dotes on you.

(*She exits into the kitchen.*)

GAIL

A beautiful black brother and sister, doing a beautiful thing.

(*She embraces* ANN.)

JEFF

Gail, I'll try to talk to Mo. I'm not certain it will do any good, but I'll try to talk to him—when he's alone— Just him and me. Okay?

GAIL

I appreciate it, Jeff.

(*She exits as* JOHN, *very intoxicated, and* DUDLEY, *still in control of himself, enter. They are arguing some philosophical point.* JOHN *sees* JEFF.)

JOHN
Jeff! Well, I'll be goddamned. Jeff!
(*He ruffles* JEFF's *hair.*)

JEFF
How you been, Pop?

JOHN
Where's your uniform?

JEFF
Dr. Stanton.

DUDLEY
You're looking fine, boy! Just fine. Skinny, but fine.

JOHN
Where's your uniform?

MATTIE
(*Coming back in, followed by* ANN, *with a cake.*)
John, you're drunk.

JOHN
Yes, my love.
(GRANDMA *comes down the stairs. She too is loaded. She's singing "Onward, Christian Soldiers."*)

JEFF
Why don't you take the load off your feet, Pop.

JOHN
Where's your uniform, Jeff? Go put it on.

JEFF
If it's all the same to you, Pop—

JOHN
I've got a theory, Dudley—Dr. Dudley Stanton—

MATTIE
Why don't you go sleep it off—

JOHN
My theory is that if you as a doctor don't try to keep the
living from dying, then you're dead yourself. You're a dead
doctor.
(GRANDMA *crosses to* JOHN *and sings directly into his ear.*)
Mrs. Brown, I have never hit an old lady in my life—

GRANDMA
Ya hit this old lady—

JOHN
And what?

GRANDMA
She's gon' jump down your throat—

JOHN
And what?

GRANDMA
Straddle your gizzard—

JOHN
And what?

GRANDMA
And gallop your brains out!
(*He picks her up and whirls her around the room, laugh-
ing.*)

JOHN

Grandma, you are the biggest fool in the world, but I sure
do love me some Grandma Wilhemina Geneva Brown.

GRANDMA

Stinking old wino.

JOHN

I love you too, Dudley—Dr. Dudley Stanton—even if you
do walk through life with a broomstick up your ass.
(*To* ANN)
And even though we just met, I loves me some Ann—sweet
fighting lady that you are. Jeff, ya got yourself a mama—a
mama who's gonna protect your flanks—a sweet fighting
lady.

JEFF

I know, Pop.
(GRANDMA *grunts disapprovingly.*)

JOHN

And my son I loves better than I love myself. My big old
big-time United States Air Force lieutenant son. He's
coming home today—

JEFF

I'm here, Pop.

JOHN

(*Really annoyed.*)
No, you ain't—you ain't here. 'Cause if you were, you'd
have on your uniform—

JEFF

I don't like to wear it, Daddy Johnny.

JOHN
Why not?

JEFF
Well, I guess—

JOHN
Spit it out.

JEFF
I feel ashamed of it. I feel that it's a kinda cop-out, Pop—
it makes me feel like a buffoon every time I put it on. I
should have burned my commission, not shown up, made
it to Canada or something. I really don't believe in this
country any more.

DUDLEY
Boy, you don't believe in the United States of America—
land of the free, home of the brave, this democratic, con-
stitutional, industrial giant?

JEFF
I don't believe in lies any more, Dr. Stanton.

DUDLEY
(*Jokingly but meaning it*)
Welcome home, Jeff. Welcome home, Brother Jeff.
(*Pats him on the back.*)

JOHN
Have I been waiting around here, waiting to see you in
that goddamn uniform—for you to— Go put it on!

JEFF
I made a vow with myself, Daddy Johnny.

JOHN
(*Getting angry.*)
It's an accomplishment, fool. How many of us ever get
there—to be an officer? God knows, this country needs to
be torn down, but don't we want it torn down for the right
to be an officer if you're able? It's an accomplishment. And
I'm proud of your accomplishment.

DUDLEY
A dubious accomplishment.

JOHN
Laugh and ridicule the damn thing all you want, goddamn
it, but recognize that it's another fist jammed through the
wall.

DUDLEY
Man, he became the protector of a system he believes
should be destroyed.

JOHN
So we're contradictions—so what else is new? That could
apply to every black man, woman, and child who ever
lived in this country. Especially the taxpayers. They been
financing the system for a long time. Besides, who ever
said we wanted total destruction anyway? If you get right
on down to the real nitty-gritty, I don't want to totally
destroy what, by rights, belongs to me anyway. I just want
to weed out the bullshit. Change the value system so that
the Waldorf has as many welfare tenants as Rockafellows.

JEFF
The Rockafellows will never allow it.

JOHN
They will if you put *them* on welfare.

DUDLEY
How in hell you gonna do that, fool?

JOHN
By finding the battlefield—like I told you—like I been
telling you—each and every motherfucker—

MATTIE
John!

JOHN
Whoever dropped from a pretty black poontang has got
to find his own battlefield and go to war. In his own way—
his own private war.

DUDLEY
All hail to the philosopher-poet.

JOHN
(*Grabbing* DUDLEY *roughly in the collar and screaming as
bass line enters.*)
I'm a poet, ya hear me, a poet! When this country—when
this world, learns the meaning of poetry—
    Don't you see, Jeff, poetry is what the revolution's all
about—never lose sight of the true purpose of the revolu-
tion, all revolutions—to restore poetry to the godhead!
Poetry is religion, the alpha and the omega, the cement
of the universe. The supereye under which every other eye
is scrutinized, and it stretches from one to infinity, from
bullshit to the beatific, the rocking horse of the human
spirit—God himself. God himself is pure distilled poetry.

DUDLEY
Bravissimo!

JOHN

Preserve the Empire State Building—if you can. It was built from over three hundred years of black poetry, 'cause sweat is poetry too, son. Kick out the money changers and reclaim it. Ain't none of us gonna be free until poetry rides a mercury-smooth silver stallion.
(*Pause.*)
Seeing you in your uniform with bars on your shoulders and them navigator wings on your chest is a kinda—
(*Bass fades.*)

DUDLEY
(*Undaunted.*)
Heresy!

JOHN
Poetry, Jeff. Black poetry.

JEFF
Pop, I didn't make it through navigator school— I washed out—flunked out—whatever.

JOHN
(*Furious.*)
My son flunked out— You lie— Go get that uniform!

JEFF
No, Daddy Johnny, no!

MATTIE
Leave him alone, Johnny.

JOHN
I'm the head of this house.

MATTIE
Ain't nobody disputing that.

JOHN
And when I ask my son—who I ain't seen but three or four times in three years—to do me one simple favor—

ANN
But if it's against his principles, Mr. Williams—

JOHN
There goes the little fighting lady, protecting your flanks.

JEFF
I don't need nobody to protect my flanks.

ANN
I know you don't, baby.

GRANDMA
(*Half high.*)
"I know you don't, baby!" Brazen hussy.

JEFF
Don't call her that again, Grandma!

GRANDMA
I calls 'em as I sees 'em. My Ben Brown told me—

MATTIE
Hush, Ma!

JEFF
I'll leave, Pop. I'll leave now—tonight—ya dig that? 'Cause I've had me enough homecoming for a lifetime.

JOHN
Ain't nobody asking you to leave—

JEFF
Ya telling me what to do like I was sweet sixteen or some-

thing. Everybody 'round here wants to tell me what to do.

MATTIE

You didn't write to us about flunking out, Jeff.

JEFF

Ya want to know why I didn't write home about it, Mama? 'Cause every single letter I got from you or Pop was tell-ing me how proud you were of your navigator son.

JOHN

We thought you were doing all right.

JEFF

You thought that because that's what you wanted to think!

JOHN

What else could we think?

JEFF

About me, Daddy Johnny, about Jeff—damn your pride! You coulda thought about me.
(*Strained pause.*)
I hated navigation! You know how I hate figures, Pop.

JOHN

You never worked hard enough!

JEFF

So you say, Daddy Johnny—'cause that's what you want to believe. "Jeff Williams is my son, everybody! Just like me. Anything I can do he can do."

JOHN

You can! It's all in how you think of yourself—

JEFF

Right, Pop, right. As a matter of fact, I may be able to do a few things you can't do. But not math, Pop. That's you, not me. Don't you dig that?

JOHN

Say what you got to say.

JEFF

Haven't I said it already? You said it yourself! We got to find our own battlefields. Don't you dig how that statement relates to what I'm saying?

JOHN

No! Hell, no, I don't. You flunked out. My boy, my boy failed. That's all I can see.

JEFF

Ya'll had a piece of my big toe, Pop. *Everybody* had a piece of my toe. Not just those white-pig instructors who kept checking and rechecking my work, 'cause I was what they called a belligerent nigger. There were only eight black officers out of three hundred in that school, and they kept telling me, "Man, you got to make it. You got to be a credit to your race."

JOHN

What's wrong with that?

JEFF

Then there was this girl I was shacking up with.

MATTIE

Shacking up!

JEFF
Shacking up, Mama!

GRANDMA
Another brazen hussy!

JEFF
She was the fox to end all foxes, Pop. An afro so soft and
spongy, until my hands felt like they were moving through
water. And she kept telling me, "Honey, we needs that
extra hundred and thirty a month flight pay to keep me
in the style to which you have made me accustomed."

JOHN
Come to the point!

JEFF
Don't you see the point, Pop? Everybody had a piece of
my nigger toe—my fine fox, my fellow black brother of-
ficers, the pig instructors, you and Mama, Pop—everybody
had a piece—but me—Jeff Williams!

JOHN
Jeff Williams is Johnny Williams's son, goddamn it!

JEFF
You mean none of me belongs to me, Pop?

JOHN
I want to see you in your uniform! Now, what is all this
talk about?

JEFF
It's about you and me and the battlefields. About who is
Jeff Williams, Pop.

JOHN

Then tell me who in the hell is he!

JEFF

A dude who hated navigation to the point where he got migraines. Who wanted to throw up on every flight—motion-sickness pills notwithstanding. Whose ears pained him from takeoff to landing. Do you know what it feels like when your ears don't clear?

MATTIE

My baby!

JEFF

(Bass enters.)

Don't baby me, Mama. I still think I'm the baddest, but I ain't—nor do I want to be a supernigger, 'cause that's all a supernigger is, a *super*nigger. Someone who spends his life trying to prove he's as good as the Man. On my last flight exam—a night celestial—I wound up eighty miles into Mexico, according to my computations, while everybody else's figures put us at Harlingen Air Force Base, Texas. We were circling the field. The sun was coming up, soft and pastel like someone had sprinkled red pepper all over the clouds. I tore off a piece of my flight log and began writing a poem. You see, Pop, I do believe in poetry. It was a simple poem—all about the awe of creation. Anyway—along came this Lieutenant Forthright—a Texas cracker whose one joke, repeated over and over again, was "Hee, haw, students, never worry about being lost. At least you knows ya'll is in the airplane. Yuk, yuk." This creep caught sight of my poem, and this big Howdy Doody grin spread all over his face, and he started laughing. This

Howdy Doody pig started laughing. This subhuman, cave-man, orangutan was laughing at something he couldn't even understand. Then he showed the poem to the other instructor orangutans, and they started laughing. And that did it, Pop. I said to myself, "This ain't my stick. What am I doing this for? What am I doing this shit for? This navigator jive ain't for me." They sent me before a board of senior officers. You see, this was the second time I'd failed my night celestial flying exam, and they gave me a flat-ass white all-American lieutenant for counsel, and you know what he told me? He told me to cop a plea, to cop a plea, Pop, to express my love of country and dedica-tion to the air force! To lick ass! That way, he said, they'd only wash me back a few months and I could still come through. But I told that board, "Let go my toe!" And they replied, "What?" You know, the way white people do when they don't believe their ears. So I screamed at the top of my voice, "Let go my nigger toe so I can stand up and be a man." . . . I guess they thought I was insane. They hemmed and hawed and cleared their throats, but they let go my toe, Mama. I had cut loose the man. Then I went right home and I cut loose my fine fox, and I cut loose my so-called black brother officers, and I felt like there was no more glue holding my shoes to the track; I felt I could almost fly, Pop, 'cause I was a supernigger no more . . . So I ain't proving nothing to nobody—white, black, blue, or polka dot—to nobody! Not even to you, Daddy Johnny . . . Mama, you give that thing—that uni-form thing to the Salvation Army or to the Goodwill or whatever, 'cause it will never have the good fortune to get on my back again.

DUDLEY
Bravo! Bravissimo!
(*Bass fades.* GRANDMA *sings "Onward, Christian Soldiers,"
and for some time no one says anything.*)

JEFF
(*Quietly*)
It's all about battlefields—just like you said, Pop.
(JOHN *pauses for an infinite time, looking at* JEFF, *then at*
MATTIE *and the others. With great deliberation he then
collects his coat and starts walking out slowly.*)

MATTIE
(*Trying to stop him.*)
John! It's Jeff's coming-home party!
(*He doesn't stop, exiting through the front door—leaving
everyone suspended in a state of sad frustration. Lights fade
as they all avoid looking at each other.*)

Act Three

It is Friday evening. DUDLEY, MATTIE, GRANDMA, *and* JEFF *are seated in the living room.* ANN *is in the kitchen busily putting away dishes. The air is very heavy. After a long pause,* JEFF *rises, moves toward the window.*

JEFF

I noticed the kids tore down the baskets on the basketball court, Ma.

MATTIE

Yeah, well, they weren't made to be swung on, that's for sure.

JEFF

Why are we so damn destructive, Ma?

MATTIE

I guess 'cause we're so mad . . . Lord, where could he be?

GRANDMA
(*Intoxicated.*)
Ain't nothing strange about a man staying away from
home. Does 'em good.

MATTIE
Mama, it's Friday. He's been gone since Saturday.

DUDLEY
Oh, he'll be all right, Mattie.

MATTIE
It's like he just disappeared—

JEFF
Mama, have you checked the police station today?

MATTIE
Five times!

DUDLEY
Well, won't do any good to worry. He's a strong, capable
man with a whole lot of sense. He's probably in some hotel
writing.

GRANDMA
You mean *drinking!*

DUDLEY
Well—both then.

MATTIE
(*On the verge of tears.*)
Anything could happen to him. All these dope fiends run-
ning 'round Harlem, banging people in the head for a
quarter. He could be laying in some vacant lot—hurt—or,
or—

JEFF
No, Mama—he's all right!

MATTIE
Six days!

DUDLEY
I'm gonna have to give you a sedative if you don't calm down, Mattie.

GRANDMA
I like sedatives myself.

DUDLEY
You starting on your medicine a little early, aren't you, Grandma?

GRANDMA
I takes my medicine whenever I need it. It opens up my chest and cuts the phlegm.

MATTIE
Poor thing—he could be seriously injured—

GRANDMA
(*Bass enters.*)
Now, that's exactly what happened to my Ben Brown. He was wild as a pine cone and as savage as a grizzly, and black! Black as a night what ain't got no moon. He'd stay out in the woods for days at a time—always come back with a mess of fish or a sack of rabbits, and possums—that man could tree a possum like he was a hound dog. I guess he was so black till they musta thought he was a shadow, creeping up on 'em.
(*Pause.*)
One day he just didn't come back.

MATTIE
Mama, do we have to hear *it* again?

GRANDMA
A load of buckshot ripped his guts right out—right out on
the ground!

MATTIE
Mama!

GRANDMA
It was an old redneck cracker named Isaiah what been
poaching on our land. Ben said he'd kill any white man
he caught hunting on our land. So there they were—both
dead—Ben musta been strangling him. I guess Isaiah
figured a load of buckshot would put a stop to him. But
there was Ben, still holding on to that cracker's throat
when we found 'em. Couldn't nothing stop my husband
from doing what he had a mind to do. They had to pry
his hands loose. Folks come from miles around to attend
his funeral. White folks too. Yes, they did. He was a king
in his own right, and they knew it. Gawdamercy, my man
was a king. And I know he's in *Glory!* Just awaiting for
his Wilhemina. I knows it.
(*Starts humming "Rock of Ages." Bass fades.*)

DUDLEY
The reason I asked to see you all tonight—well—well—
because Mattie and I have something very serious to discuss
with you.

MATTIE
Do they have to know, Dudley?

DUDLEY
It's only fair that they should know, Mattie. Mattie is going

to have to be hospitalized. I guess that's why Johnny hasn't
been home— I guess he's off somewhere—brooding.

MATTIE

Dudley! You promised me you wouldn't tell him—

DUDLEY

I made a decision, Mattie. It was either keep my promise
to you or prepare Johnny ahead of time for what might
kill him—if he heard it too sudden-like . . .

MATTIE

Then you're responsible— If anything's happened to him
—you're responsible.

DUDLEY

I made a judgment—

JEFF

Will somebody please tell me what's going on?

DUDLEY

Jeff, we got the report today. Mattie's got, well, several
growths—malignant growths. Mattie's got cancer.

MATTIE

There you go again—about as gentle as a sledgehammer.

JEFF

How serious?

DUDLEY

Very serious, but not hopeless—the location prevents re-
moval, but radium treatments might arrest the—

MATTIE

Jeff, you don't see me upset, do you, son?

JEFF
(*Cupping her face in his hands lovingly.*)
Mama!

MATTIE
I'm gonna die—that's all there is to it.

GRANDMA
No such thing! You know Dudley here's a cockeyed
quack—

MATTIE
Mama, the only thing I'm worried about is the where-
abouts of my man.

JEFF
But you can't think negative like that—
(GRANDMA *sings loudly,* "*For His eye is on the sparrow,
and I know He watches me.*")

MATTIE
Hush, Mama.
(ANN *comes to the door. Bass enters.*)
Now, what old negative? Look at me! I've had a full life
with an extraordinary man who fell upon me and fed my
soul like manna from heaven—bless him, God bless him
wherever he is— And you—where could I get a finer-
looking, stronger-looking, more loving son than my Jeff?
And I'll be around to see you marry Ann—a gift to you,
Jeff, and don't you abuse her. I got my mother beside me,
still alive and kicking. And Dudley Stanton—a mainstay—
your father's and my spiritual brother—

DUDLEY
Thank you, sweetheart—

MATTIE

No, Dudley! Thank you. Now, what old negative think-
ing? If Johnny were to come through that door right now,
I'd be the happiest woman in God's creation—and like my
Johnny says, "Lord, I don't feel noways tired—I could go
on for another century."

JEFF
(*Very upset.*)
You will, Mama. You will.

MATTIE

But it's my time, baby. I guess maybe I've done whatever
He put me here to do.
(*There is a knock on the front door.* ANN *answers it. It is*
MO *and* GAIL. ANN *shows them into the living room.*)

MO

Dr. Stanton! Mrs. Williams— Grandma—

MATTIE

How've you been, Li'l Mo? Lord, you sure have grown.

GAIL

Mrs. Williams—everybody—
(GRANDMA *grunts.*)

MO

I got to see you, Jeff.

JEFF
Is it important?

MO
I need your help, Jeff.

JEFF

Let's go into the kitchen. I'll be right back, Mama.

(JEFF, MO, GAIL, *and* ANN *move toward kitchen. Living-room conversation continues.*)

MATTIE

Looks like rain.

GRANDMA

I sure hate this dirty city when it rains—looks like a cess-pool.

DUDLEY

One thing good about rain in February—it means an early spring.

JEFF

(*From the kitchen*)

Look, man, I know I promised Gail—but that's gonna have to wait. My folks are in heavy trouble.

MO

Yeah, I heard about your father.

ANN

We just found out Mrs. Williams has cancer.

GAIL

Oh, Jeff, I'm so sorry.

MO

Wow, me too, man—I see what you mean. Wow!

MATTIE

(*From the living room*)

Don't you think—well—we could go on without Jeff, Dudley? He's just a child.

DUDLEY
He's a man now, Mattie, and with Grandma getting up
there and Johnny—taking it so hard—

GRANDMA
Who's getting up where? A body ain't no older than their
toes, and mine twinkle a damn sight better than yours—

DUDLEY
When you've had your medicine.

GAIL
(*From the kitchen*)
How serious is it, Jeff?

ANN
It's inoperable. The only hope is radium treatment.

MO
I'm sorry, man. I really am.

JEFF
Thanks.

MATTIE
(*From living room*)
Mama, sing that song for me.

GRANDMA
Which song, daughter?

MATTIE
"Rock of Ages."
(GRANDMA *begins singing soothingly.* MATTIE *joins her from
time to time.*)

MO
(*From kitchen*)
All them years we was running together, Mrs. Williams
was like a mother to me too, remember, Jeff?

JEFF
Yeah.

MO
I guess that changes things 'round. I wouldn't want to put
more weight on you now, especially behind news like that.

ANN
What is the problem, Gail?

GAIL
There's a stool pigeon in the organization. It's gotta be
either Chips, Skeeter, or Al.

ANN
Oh no.

GAIL
If we don't find him out quick, everything's liable to blow
up in our faces. Remember what I told y'all 'bout that cop
Buckley?

ANN
What can Jeff do?

GAIL
Mo's laying a trap tonight where the stoolie's gonna hafta
phone his boss. He'll hafta do it from either the pool-hall
phone next to headquarters, or the bar phone down the
street. Mo's got both phones bugged, ready to be moni-
tored. I'll be listening in the pool-hall basement, and we

wanted Jeff to cover the phone in the bar. Jeff's the only person we can trust.

MO

What about it, Jeff?

JEFF

(*Angrily*)

I got no time for this cloak-and-dagger shit—my folks are hurting, man, didn't you hear?

MO

Okay, man. Okay, I dig.

ANN

What about me?

JEFF

(*Adamantly*)

Hell, no. I won't let you or my family get implicated in this shit—

ANN

Jeff, I don't intend to get implicated—but what Gail and Mo are asking doesn't seem unreasonable. Remember?—my brothers were betrayed once, Jeff. My father is still in prison as a result. Nine years with still no release in sight. No matter what you and I might think about Mo's activities, he certainly does not deserve betrayal. I could not live with myself knowing that I had an opportunity to help and didn't.

MO

Thanks for the offer, baby. But I'm afraid it's no good. What has to be done and where it's gotta happen, a woman would only draw suspicion.

JEFF
How long would it take, Mo?

MO
No more than an hour's time, Jeff. All together, you should be back here three hours from right now. I promise you, Jeff, it'll be no sweat. I just need to know, you dig?

JEFF
Why you sure he'll make contact?

MO
He's gotta. Tonight is the night of our big thing, Jeff. I'm ordering a change of plan at the last minute that's gonna make the rat hafta contact the pigs. Meanwhile, nobody but me knows that I'm crossing everybody up by following through with my original plan. Nobody's gonna get hurt, Jeff, just some property damaged. While everybody is on their way to the police station, I'll be headed—

JEFF
I don't want to know, Mo. I'll monitor the phone for you, but I don't want to know nothing. Don't crowd me, Mo, you understand?

MO
That's cool, Jeff.

JEFF
This is as far as I go, Mo.

MO
I gotcha, Brother Jeff. I dig.

ANN
And I will sit with Gail at the pool hall.

JEFF
No!

ANN
She shouldn't be alone, Jeff.

JEFF
I SAID NO!

MO
It's safe, Jeff. I swear. You know I wouldn't have my woman doing anything that would put her in a trick. No jeopardy, man, I promise.

MATTIE
(*From living room*)
What time you got, Dudley?

DUDLEY
Five after seven.

MATTIE
You think he's had his dinner?

DUDLEY
Sure, sweetheart. Keep singing, Grandma.

JEFF
(*From the kitchen*)
All right, Ann.

MO
Groovy. Make it to the bar about 8:45, Jeff. Take a cab so you'll be seen as little as possible. The bartender, a buddy of mine, will take you to the setup. About the same time Jeff leaves here, Gail will pick you up outside, Ann. Okay, we'll split now—by the back door. So we won't disturb—

Like I said, Jeff, I really am sorry about Mrs. Williams. I really mean it.

JEFF
Yeah, later, Mo.

MO
Okay.
(MO *and* GAIL *exit out the kitchen door.* JEFF *and* ANN *return to the living room.*)

MATTIE
What happened to Mo and his girl?

JEFF
They went out the back, Mama.
(*There is an awkward silence.*)

DUDLEY
Jeff, Mattie will be admitted to the hospital on Monday.

MATTIE
Couldn't I be treated at home, Dudley? Ann's a nurse. She could—

ANN
You need special equipment, Mrs. Williams, but of course I'll be your nurse.

MATTIE
Would you, Ann? I hate those nurses at Harlem. They're so indifferent and snooty.

JEFF
Goddamn!

GRANDMA

Watch your mouth! Can't even pee straight and using that kind of language.

(*There's a second sound at the back door.* JOHN: *"I'm all right! I can make it!"* JEFF *and* ANN *rush to open the door, exiting. We hear voices outside—*MO *and* GAIL *explaining.* JOHN *enters, assisted by* JEFF *and* ANN. *He has a week's growth of beard. His eyes have the deep-socket look of an alcoholic who's been on a substantial bender. His overall appearance is gaunt and shoddy. His clothes are filthy and wrinkled. He obviously smells. His hands have a slight tremor. There is a deep gash above his left eye. Bass enters.* JOHN *is helped into a chair,* MATTIE *embracing him.*)

MATTIE

Johnny, sweet Johnny! We've been so worried about you.

JOHN

Don't, Mattie! I smell something awful.

DUDLEY

Move, Mattie. Let me take a look at that cut.
(*Moves* MATTIE *aside.*)
Jeff, bring my bag. It's in the hallway there.
(JEFF *exits to hallway.*)
Hand me a towel, Grandma.

GRANDMA

Old wino, nigger.

DUDLEY

Wet it with cold water. Maybe we can stop the bleeding.

ANN

I'll hold it, Dr. Stanton.

DUDLEY

Good girl.

(*She presses the folded paper towel to* JOHNNY's *cut.*)

JOHN

Fighting lady Ann. I sure needed me a fighting lady out there. You shoulda seen me, Mattie, when them young hoods jumped me.

MATTIE

I saw you, baby. Every second.

JOHN

I was like a cornered wildcat. I was battlin' 'em to a draw. Then Li'l Mo and his fighting lady came up.

DUDLEY

It's a bird, it's a plane, it's a Supercullud Guy!

JOHN

Super Black Man, sicklehead. I ain't been hanging out with them militant winos for nothing.

DUDLEY

Folks, take a look at an aging African warrior, trying to make a comeback.

JOHN

(*Singing to a made-up tune.*)
When I get home to Africa
I'll buy myself a mango.
Grab myself a monkey gal
And do the monkey tango.

DUDLEY

When'd you eat last?

JOHN

Niggers used to sing that to make fun of Marcus Garvey.
Can you imagine. The great Marcus Garvey.

DUDLEY

Answer my question! When was the last time you had a
decent meal?

JOHN

Wednesday. Or was it Tuesday?

DUDLEY

What are you trying to do, Johnny?
(JEFF *returns with the bag.*)

ANN

I'll do it.
(*She swabs the wound and bandages it.*)

MATTIE

Where've you been, baby?

JOHN

In the desert, Mattie. Out in the desert, like Christ, talking
to myself.

GRANDMA

Christ was talking to the devil, ya old wino.

JOHN

Same difference. But I took care of the old bastard. I said,
Get thee behind me, Prince of Darkness! Then I got thirsty
and came home. I wanted to see me some angels.

JEFF

Pop, you okay now? I mean, for real?

JOHN

Yeah, Jeff. Welcome home, son. My son is really home. And I'm happy he's found his battlefield.

MATTIE

You won't do it again, will you, Johnny? If something's troubling you, let's talk about it. Okay? Now promise!

JOHN

I was all right, Mattie—really. Dulcey gave me a room over her store. I told her I wanted to think—to write some poetry. I wanted to write a love poem—to you, Mattie. Words are like precious jewels, did you know that? But I couldn't find any jewels precious enough to match you, Mattie. So I took to drinking, and before I knew it, I was drunk all the time. I couldn't stop. Then yesterday these little men came to visit me—about one foot tall. They both had a T-shirt on with a zero on the chest. And they carried two little satchels. I asked 'em what they were carrying in 'em, and they opened up the satchels, and they were empty. I asked them their names, and they said, "The Nothing Brothers." That's when I figured it was time to go home.

DUDLEY

Delirium tremens—D.T.'s from not eating.

JOHN

Whatever. I knew it was time to come home. I knew it was Friday too. Dudley told me he'd have some information for me on Friday.
(*Tense silence.*)

DUDLEY
(*Avoiding it.*)
What kind of information?

JEFF
We all know, Pop.

JOHN
You all know? Then—

DUDLEY
Mattie will be admitted Monday morning.
(*At this point,* JOHN *goes berserk. Screams at the top of his voice. Racing around the room, whipping with an imaginary whip, and screaming, "Get out, get out, you motherfuckers. Get out of my father's house!" He falls to the floor—somewhat exhausted, looks up as if to heaven. Bass counterpoint increases.*)

JOHN
You son-of-a-bitch, why do you keep fucking with me? What do you want from me, you bastard?

MATTIE
Johnny, don't talk like that. That's blasphemy.

JOHN
He keeps fucking with me, Mattie. When I was a kid, the bigger kids used to always pick on me. I had to fight every day. They said it was because I was a smart aleck.
(*To the heavens*)
Is that why, you bastard, 'cause I'm a smart aleck?

MATTIE
You can't talk to Him like that. He'll turn His back on you.

JOHN

You know what I'm gonna do on Judgment Day? I'm gonna grab that motherfucker by the throat and squeeze and squeeze and squeeze until I get an answer.

MATTIE

He doesn't have to give you an answer. I thought you said, "Get thee behind me—" I thought you took care a Satan!

JOHN

(*Breaks into tears.*)

I tried, Mattie. I tried—you don't know how fucking hard I tried.

MATTIE

(*Embraces him.*)

I know, baby. I see you every second.

JOHN

You shoulda let me whip 'em out, Mattie. You shoulda let me whip out the bullshit.

MATTIE

We weren't made that way, baby.

JOHN

You shoulda let me whip out the money changers. You deserve so much more than this nothing. I wanted to do so much for you, Mattie.

MATTIE

I got *you*, baby. I got the kindest, sweetest man in the world. I got the Rolls-Royce, baby.

JOHN

I coulda done it, Mattie. God knows, I coulda done it!

MATTIE

I know, baby. I put it on you. I stopped you and I'm sorry.
I'm sorry. Will you forgive me, sweet baby? Please forgive
me! I was selfish, Johnny. I've been so goddam happy!
All I ever cared about was seeing you walk, stumble, or
stagger through that door. I only complained because I
felt I should say something—but I never meant it, Johnny,
I never meant a word. You couldn't have given me nothing
more, baby. I'da just keeled over and died from too much
happiness. Just keeled over and died.

(*Lights begin to dim as bass rises. Music remains as long
as it takes actors to exit and get into place for next scene.
When lights finally rise again,* MATTIE *and* DUDLEY *are
sitting in living room,* MATTIE *under heavy sedation, inter-
mittently knitting, nodding from time to time.* DUDLEY *is
watching TV, smoking a cigar. Silence ensues for a long
time. Finally* MATTIE *addresses* DUDLEY.)

MATTIE

What'd you give me, Dudley? Sure is strong. Can hardly
keep my head up.

DUDLEY

Do you feel any pain?

MATTIE

Not now.

DUDLEY

Then it's doing its job. You'll rest good when you go to
bed.

MATTIE

Which can't be too long from now. The way I'm feeling.

(JOHN *appears at the top of the stairs; descends slowly, as he is absorbed in reading some pages. He enters the living room and announces quietly . . .*)

JOHN
I finished it.

MATTIE
What?

JOHN
A poem I been working on, Mattie. It's your poem, Mattie. "The River Niger." It ain't a love poem, but it's for you, sugar, dedicated to my superbitch, Mattie Jean Williams.

DUDLEY
Read it to us, nigger.
(ANN *and* GAIL *are seen entering the back door.* JEFF *too.* JOHN *begins to read, and bass begins low with African motif and gradually rises.* JEFF *and girls begin to engage in conversation, but desist when they hear* JOHN. *They drift to living room.*)

JOHN
I am the River Niger—hear my waters!
I am totally flexible.
I am the River Niger—hear my waters!
My waters are the first sperm of the world.
When the earth was but a faceless whistling embryo,
Life burst from my liquid kernels like popcorn.
Hear my waters—rushing and popping in muffled finger-
    drum staccato.
It is life you hear, stretching its limbs in my waters—

I am the River Niger! Hear my waters!
When the Earth Mother cracked into continents,
I was vomited from the cold belly of the Atlantic
To slip slyly into Africa
From the underside of her brow.
I see no—
Hear no—
Speak no evil,
But I know.
I gossip with the crocodile
And rub elbows with the river horse.
I have swapped morbid jokes with the hyena
And heard his dry cackle at twilight.
I see no—
Hear no—
Speak no evil,
But I know.

I am the River Niger—hear my waters!
Hear, I say, hear my waters, man!
They is Mammy-tammys, baby.
I have lapped at the pugnacious hips of brown mamas.
Have tapped on the doors of their honeydews, yeah!
I have shimmered like sequins
As they sucked me over their blueberry tongues,
As they sung me to sleep in the glittering afternoon, yeah!
I have washed the red wounds of clay-decorated warriors—
Bad, bad dudes who smirked at the leopard.
I have cast witches from gabbling babies, yeah!
Have known the warm piss from newly circumcized boys.
Have purified the saliva from sun-drenched lions—
Do you hear me talking?

I am the River Niger!
I came to the cloudy Mississippi
Over keels of incomprehensible woe.
I ran 'way to the Henry Hudson
Under the sails of ragged hope.
I am the River Niger,
Transplanted to Harlem
From the Harlem River Drive.
Hear me, my children—hear my waters!
I sleep in your veins.
I see no—
Hear no—
Speak no evil,
But I know, and I know that you know.
I flow to the ends of your spirit.
Hold hands, my children, and I will flow to the ends of the
*   earth,*
And the whole world will hear my waters.
I am the River Niger! Don't deny me!
Do you hear me? Don't deny me!
(Pause. Bass fades.)

MATTIE
That's very beautiful, Johnny.

JEFF
Yeah, Pop, that's pretty nice.

DUDLEY
(Sarcastically)
Interesting!

JOHN
Ya monkey chaser.

JEFF
How you feeling, Mama?

MATTIE
Okay, I guess. A little woozy, but I'm going to bed now, and I couldn't think of a better time than after Johnny's poem. Thank you, dear.

JOHN
Be up soon, Mattie.

MATTIE
Take your time.

DUDLEY
Yeah, I'd better get home, too.

JEFF
Good night, Mama.

ANN and GAIL
Good night, Mrs. Williams.

MATTIE
Good night.
(*She exits.*)
(GRANDMA *enters, humming "Rock of Ages." They pass each other on the stairs.*)
Good night, Mama.

GRANDMA
Sleep tight! Don't let the bedbugs bite.
(MATTIE *exits, shaking her head.* GRANDMA *hums throughout this scene. She comes into the living room.*)

JEFF
How ya feel, Pop?

JOHN
Fine! Fine, still a little shaky, but all right.

JEFF
Ya got any booze, Pop?

JOHN
No, I'm drying out. Doctor's orders.

GRANDMA
Where's the *TV Guide?*
(*She searches for it.*)

DUDLEY
(*Finding it underneath him.*)
Oh, here it is, Mrs. Brown. I was sitting on it.

GRANDMA
It was under you all this time?

DUDLEY
I guess so.

GRANDMA
Then let it cool off a little bit before you give it to me.

JEFF
(*To* ANN *and* GAIL)
Let's make it into the kitchen.

ANN
I'm still cold from outside.

DUDLEY
(*To* JEFF)
Has it started raining yet?

JEFF
It's raining and snowing at the same time.
(*They move to kitchen.*)

JOHN
See, Dudley, life's full of contradictions.

DUDLEY
Ain't nothing contradictory about nature, man. Nature is everything. It's human beings who are contradictions.

JOHN
Well, ain't human beings a part of nature?

DUDLEY
(*Seriously*)
Guess so, now that you mention it.

JOHN
That's why we're so messed up. We forget that we're just a part of nature.
(*Pause.*)
Put on the TV, Dudley.

DUDLEY
I should be going home.

JOHN
Relax, man.
(DUDLEY *switches on the TV*.)

JEFF
(*From the kitchen*)
What'd *you* hear, Gail?

GAIL
Nothing but Skeeter, making a horse connection.

ANN
We thought it might be a code, but it sounded innocent enough.

GAIL
What about you?

JEFF
I heard something all right. But I couldn't identify the voice. The bartender was no help; he was somewhere else when the call was made.

GAIL
What did the caller say?

JEFF
Plan B.

GAIL
That's all—"Plan B"?

JEFF
Right. And the voice on the other end said, "You sure?" The caller said, "Yes—Plan B."

GAIL
You couldn't recognize the voice?

JEFF
No, but I might if I heard it again.

GAIL

I shouldn't have let you talk me into coming here. Mo
might need me.

JEFF

Calm down, baby. We'll hear soon.

GAIL

But something might have happened.

ANN

He wanted you to come with us.

JEFF

Stop worrying, Mo's all right.

GAIL

I can't help it . . .
(*She attempts to calm herself, crossing to the back door
and looking out.*)
It sure is beginning to come down. Beginning to stick.

ANN

I've been away from South Africa for a long time, but I
still can't get used to snow.

GAIL

Snow makes everything so quiet. It's spooky.

GRANDMA

(*Entering the kitchen.*)
Ya wants some spirits?

JEFF

We sure do, Grandma.

GRANDMA
Turn your backs.
(*She produces a bottle of Old Grand-dad from her new hiding place on top of the cabinet—pours each of them a drink.*)
The way things been happening 'round here today, a body needs some spirits. Here! Besides, this child's so fidgety—
(*Referring to* GAIL.)
—done got my phlegm acting up again.
(GRANDMA *downs hers. For a second they watch in amazement—then down theirs. There is a noise at the back door.* JEFF *goes to the door.*)

JEFF
It's Mo and Skeets.
(*Opens door.* MO *drags* SKEETER *in. It's obvious he's been hurt.*)

MO
Pigs are swarming all over headquarters!
(DUDLEY *enters, followed closely by* JOHN. DUDLEY *examines* SKEETER.)

DUDLEY
Gunshot wound. What's going on 'round here? Bring me my bag, Ann. You're very lucky, young man—no bones broken. Put a tourniquet on that arm, Ann, while I clean it out.
(ANN *and* DUDLEY *work on* SKEETER. JEFF *pulls* MO *into the living room.*)

JEFF
Why in the hell did you bring him here?

MO

I figured Dr. Stanton would be here—

JEFF

I told you I don't want my family implicated in this shit—
Why didn't you take him to your place?

MO

(JOHN *comes to the door.*)
I live over headquarters! The pigs—

JEFF

Oh, shit—shit—what happened?

MO

It's stupid—stupid. I mean, we had just crossed the street.
I mean, we were just walking 'round the fence when this
pig started blowing his whistle and yelling at us.

JEFF

They musta been alerted.

MO

Fucking Skeeter panicked—started running—what the
hell am I supposed to do? I'm carrying a tote bag with four
sticks of dynamite. So I start running too. Next thing I
know, there're four pigs chasing us. One fires and spins
Skeets clean 'round. Skeets is screaming and shit, and
they're gaining, so I blast off a couple and knock trigger-
happy on his ass.

JEFF

What—you crazy motherfucker, coming here after that?

JOHN

You mean, they just started shooting? You didn't shoot
first?

MO
Why would we do that?

JOHN
You sure?

MO
I don't want to hurt nobody if I can help it, Mr. Williams.

JOHN
You think he's dead?

MO
I don't know. He hit the ground so hard I could almost feel it.

JOHN
I sure hope you killed the bastard. But if you call yourself a revolutionary, then you supposed to know where you gonna take your wounded. Takes more'n wearing a goddamn beret.

DUDLEY
(*From the kitchen*)
Yeah! Why don't I set up another office over here?
(*There is a wild banging on the front door.* JEFF *answers the door.* AL *enters, followed closely by* CHIPS.)

JEFF
(*Angrily*)
What's going on?

AL
There are wall-to-wall pigs at headquarters. And Mo said—

JEFF
(*To* MO)
And you told them to come here if that happened—
(*Silence.*)
Didn't you? Didn't you? Didn't I tell you not to crowd me,
ya stupid bastard?

MO
I was wrong, Jeff. I'm sorry.

JEFF
You're sorry.
(JEFF *leaps on* MO *and is separated by* JOHN.)
I'll kill him, Pop, so help me. I'll kill him!

JOHN
You'll wake up your mother.
(*In the next second, a confusion of sirens and police
whistles—lights shining through the front windows and
the back door, and a policeman on a bullhorn.*)

LIEUTENANT STAPLES'S VOICE
(*From outside*)
This is Lieutenant Staples from the Thirty-second Police
Precinct. We know you are in there and who's in there. We
gotcha front and back, plus men on the roof. You got five
minutes to throw out your weapons and come out of there.
And let me remind whoever else is in there not to harbor
criminals from the law. You got five minutes. If there're
innocent people in there, their blood will be on your
hands.

JOHN
Give me those goddamn guns.
(*Pause.*)

Come on, come on! They can't prove a thing—except those guns. Dudley, get Skeeter's. Come on, Mo, give it to me.

(MO *hesitates, but gives it to him.*)

CHIPS
Al's the one, Mo. A fucking Judas faggot.

AL
You lie!

CHIPS
There were cops everywhere. You said not to do nothing when we got to the police station until you and Skeeter showed, right? Well, when you didn't show, he ran across the street and deliberately bumped into one of 'em—

AL
He's lying.

CHIPS
And whispered something in his ear. Next thing I know, every pig and his mother is jumping into a car—that's when it hit me you was pulling a trick, and the state office building plan was still on.

AL
I didn't have a damn thing to do with that.

CHIPS
You shoulda heard the squawk boxes, "State office building —emergency—emergency." The block was vacant inside of a minute.

AL
You're not believing this shit?

CHIPS

Then he tried to shake me, Mo. Caught a cab, and you know what he told him? Told him to go to the state office building.

AL

I gave him the address of headquarters.

CHIPS

You lie, nigger. I overheard you.

SKEETER
(*Coming out of the kitchen.*)
And the way you keep questioning me about Buckley—

MO

Why didn't you tell me about that?

AL

He's your informer, Mo. He'd do anything for horse.
(*Pause.*)
He told them pigs to go to the state office building. He's the one.

MO

He was with me.

JEFF
(*To* AL)
It was you. I heard you.

AL

Heard me what?

JEFF

The phone—you phoned. It was your voice. You said, "B."

The voice at the other end said, "Are you sure?" and you repeated, "B!"

AL
That don't prove nothing— Skeeter left too—we both went to the phone.

JEFF
Okay, if it wasn't you then, suppose I were to tell you I killed Buckley?

AL
What do you know about Buckley?

JEFF
I did it. I killed him.

AL
How'd he die?

JEFF
Two slugs in the chest.

AL
What caliber?

JEFF
Forty-five. I stole it from the air force.

AL
Don't shit me. Buckley was killed almost a month ago. Ya only been here a week.

JEFF
What makes you so sure?

MO
What are you doing, Jeff?

JEFF

I was released from active duty exactly one month from last Friday.

AL

Bullshit!

JEFF

Wanta see my release papers?

ANN

Jeff!

JEFF

Stay out of it, Ann!
(*Fumbles through wallet and gives* AL *his release papers.* AL *reads them.*)

AL

(*Pulling out his revolver.*)
All right, stand still, all of you! I took this assignment for one reason and one reason only, to find out who killed Buckley. And now I know.
(*To* JEFF)
You killed Buckley. He was worth ten of you Brillo heads. Now his friends out there are gonna take this place apart, and all of you are in trouble, you hear. You motherfuckers, fucking up the country with your slogans and your jive-ass threats. Militants, ain't that a bitch. Black cripples, trying to scale a mountain. I hate the smell of you assholes.

MO

Jeff's lying, can't you see that? I killed Buckley.

SKEETER

I did it.

CHIPS
I did it.

AL
No, no, it fits. It fits. I know where each of you mothers were when Buckley was killed. None of you coulda done it. He did it. Why didn't I think of good old Jeff? All I heard about was good old Jeff. Jeff this—Jeff that—till you bastards staged your phony scene to throw me off the track when he got here.

MO
Don't be stupid. It was an outside job.

AL
(*To* JEFF)
Yeah—him.

ANN
What are you doing, Jeff? You know you were with me that whole month in Canada!
(*This causes* AL *to pause for a moment in frozen doubt.* JOHN *seizes the opportunity to raise the gun still in his hand, pointing it at* AL.)

JOHN
Drop it, son.
(AL *whirls and shoots. There is an exchange of gun play between the two men.* AL *goes down, killed instantly.* JOHN *also goes down, mortally wounded.*)

JEFF
(*Rushing to his father's side, followed closely by* DUDLEY.)
POP!

JOHN

The guns, Jeff—put 'em in the drain in the basement. Al's still holding his? Good.

JEFF

Pop!

JOHN

Hurry, you don't want Daddy Johnny to die for nothing, do you?
(JEFF *grabs* SKEETER's *and* CHIPS's, *tries to take* MO's.)
No! We need Mo's—this is yours, ain't it, Mo?

MO

Yes, sir.

JOHN

Go on, son.
(JEFF *exits.*)
(*To* DUDLEY, *who's been trying to get at* JOHN's *wound*)
Don't worry about that, ya monkey chaser. They'll be in here in a second.

DUDLEY

You're hurt, man. Ann—my bag—
(ANN *starts off.*)

JOHN

Fuck your bag, Dudley. Go to the door—tell that Lieutenant Staples—tell him—to give us five more minutes—just five more—then he can make his arrests—

DUDLEY

You'll die if I don't—

JOHN
I'll die anyway. Do as I say! Before they shoot up Mattie's house.
(ANN *comes back with bag, starts preparing dressings.* JEFF *returns.* MATTIE *appears at the top of the stairs.*)

MATTIE
(*Extremely drowsy.* JEFF *and* GAIL *run to her, the rest are stupefied.*)
I had a dream, and I heard this noise in the middle of it.

DUDLEY
(*Waving a handkerchief out the front door and shouting.*)
Lieutenant Staples—Lieutenant Staples.

STAPLES'S VOICE
This is Lieutenant Staples—what's going on in there?

DUDLEY
I'm Dr. Dudley Stanton—next-door neighbor. A man's been seriously wounded in here. Call an ambulance.

STAPLES'S VOICE
Throw out your guns.

DUDLEY
I think it would be best for you to see the situation for yourself.

JOHN
Good boy, Dudley. They don't care nothing 'bout niggers killing themselves nohow.

DUDLEY
(*To* STAPLES)
Both weapons are secured. I have them. Give us five minutes, then come in.

STAPLES'S VOICE
If anyone tries to escape, my men have orders to shoot—

MATTIE
What on earth's going on?

DUDLEY
No one will. I give my word. Five minutes.
(*Closes the door.*)

CHIPS
We *got* to get outta here!

MO
Shut up, and stay tight!

JEFF
(*To* MO)
Do you see what you brought in here tonight?
(*Leaps for* MO *once again.*)

JOHN
Jeff, stop it. Don't make a mockery out of my death. Sit down, all of you, and listen to me.

MATTIE
(*For the first time realizing* JOHN's *hurt.*)
Johnny! Johnny!

JOHN
Keep Mattie away, Dudley—keep her away—

DUDLEY
(*Restraining her.*)
Try and be calm, Mattie.

JOHN
Wipe off the handle on Mo's gun, Jeff.
(JEFF *does it.*)
Okay, now give it to me.
(*He grips the gun firmly several times.*)
I don't want nobody's fingerprints on it but mine.

MATTIE
Johnny, you're bleeding—

JOHN
(*With savage power*)
Mattie, I love ya, Mattie. I ain't got much life left.

MATTIE
Johnny, no!

JOHN
I got to get our children straight before I go—now be my superbitch and shut the fuck up.
(MATTIE *understands and obeys.*)
Now you youngbloods listen to me. Here's the story: I am the real leader of the organization—ya got me. I was with Skeeter when he got shot. I fired the shot which hit the cop at the office building. I made it back here—found out that Al here is a Judas, and we had a shoot-out. The rest of you have never owned a gun—only your leader—me! Ya got that?

GRANDMA
(*Drunk, and in a state of shock, comes strangely alive. She*

thinks JOHN *is her Ben. She rushes up and falls at* JOHN's
knees.)
BEN—BEN BROWN!
(*Reaches for* JOHN's *gun.*)
Gimme that shotgun.
(MATTIE *blocks her.*)

MATTIE
(*Very calm and solemn, almost eerie.*)
No, Mama.

GRANDMA
I'll just shoot right into the crowd, daughter. See 'em, look
at their faces! They's glad to see my Ben dead. Lawda-
mercy! He's dead!
(*Crying from an ancient wound.*)
Gimme that shotgun, child. Ten for one, ten for one—my
man is a king—you crackers—ya dirty old redneck crack-
ers.
(*Breaks into "Rock of Ages." Bass counterpoint seeps in.*)

JOHN
Hear that, Mattie. The old battle-ax finally gave me a
compliment. Where's my Mattie? Let me see my Mattie.
(MATTIE's *let through. They embrace.*)

MATTIE
I'm with you every second, baby.

JOHN
I knew she'd slip one day. I'm sorry, Mattie.

MATTIE
What for, baby?

JOHN

I'm cheating ya, honey—going first this way.

MATTIE

Hush now!

JOHN

Don't suffer long, honey. Just give up and take my hand.
The children—the children will be all right now.
(*Pause.*)
Look at Dr. Dudley Stanton down there. Trying to save
my life. Ain't that a bitch! See what a big old fake you've
been all along. Don't worry, Dudley—fighting lady Ann—
Jeff—ya got a fighting lady to protect your flanks, son—
don't worry, I don't feel nothing now. Just sweetness—a
sweet sweetness.

DUDLEY

Your poems—I'll get 'em published.

JOHN

Fuck them poems—this is poetry, man—what I feel right
here and now. This sweetness. Sing on, Grandma.
(*Pause. He shivers.*)
I found it, Dudley—I found it.

DUDLEY

What, Johnny?

JOHN

My battlefield—my battlefield, man! I was a bitch too, ya
monkey chaser. See my shit! I got two for the price of one.

DUDLEY

Yeah, chief.
(JOHN *dies. Pause.*)

CHIPS
(*Whimpering.*)
Oh God, oh my God!

MATTIE
Shut up! And tell it like Johnny told ya. He ain't gonna
die for nothing, 'cause you ain't gonna let him! Jeff—open
the door, son! Tell 'em to come on in here!
(JEFF *crosses to the door.*)
And you better not fuck up!